Collins

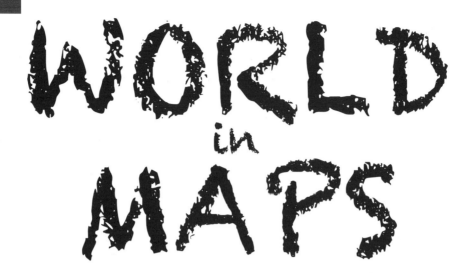

WORLD in MAPS

Editorial advisor Dr. Stephen Scoffham

CW00954026

Contents

Free activities available at www.collins.co.uk/InMaps

The Solar System

The Earth is one of eight planets that circle the sun. Mercury and Venus are hotter than the Earth because they are closer to the sun. Jupiter and Saturn are colder because they are further away. They are made up of great masses of frozen gas.

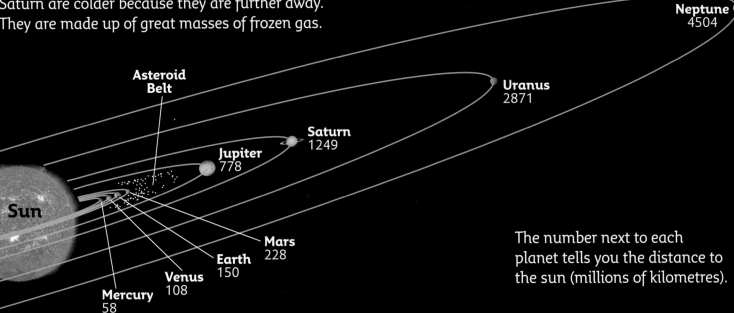

Neptune 4504

Uranus 2871

Asteroid Belt

Saturn 1249

Jupiter 778

Mars 228

Earth 150

Venus 108

Mercury 58

Sun

The number next to each planet tells you the distance to the sun (millions of kilometres).

What causes day and night?

The Earth spins as it travels through space. It takes 24 hours for the Earth to rotate once. The diagrams show how the UK passes from day to night. They show the Earth from directly above the North Pole.

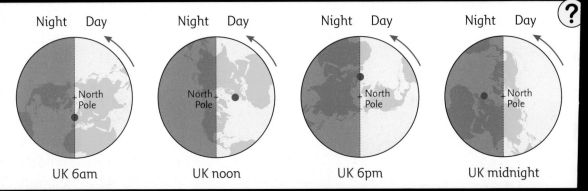

Night Day	Night Day	Night Day	Night Day
North Pole	North Pole	North Pole	North Pole
UK 6am	UK noon	UK 6pm	UK midnight

The Seasons

The Earth's axis is tilted. In the summer places are tilted towards the sun. In the winter they are tilted away from the sun. It takes a year for the Earth to complete its orbit and for the pattern of the seasons to be completed.

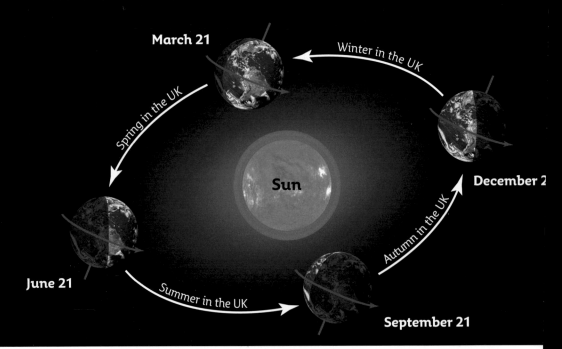

March 21

Winter in the UK

Spring in the UK

Sun

December 2

June 21

Autumn in the UK

Summer in the UK

September 21

The Earth's surface

The Earth is a very special planet. Air and water mix at just the right temperatures for animals and plants to live. No other planet is quite the same.

On Earth, air and water are always moving.

The moon is still and lifeless.

Life on Earth

It has taken a huge time for life to evolve on Earth. The first traces of life go back about 1000 million years. Fish date back about 440 million years. It seems that human beings may have developed about four million years ago. The oldest human remains come from Ethiopia and other parts of Africa.

How life began

Look at the diagram to see how many million years ago each plant or creature developed.

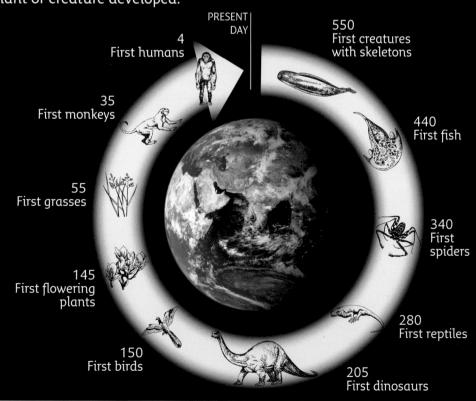

PRESENT DAY
4 First humans
550 First creatures with skeletons
35 First monkeys
440 First fish
55 First grasses
340 First spiders
145 First flowering plants
280 First reptiles
150 First birds
205 First dinosaurs

Activities

➤ Make drawings of different creatures. Arrange them along a piece of string to make a timeline of life on Earth.
➤ Make a large class model of the solar system.
www.earthfromspace.sci.edu
www.youtube.com (Earth from space)

3

Mapping the World

How do people draw world maps?

Globes are the only way to show the true size and shape of the continents. However, flat maps are often more convenient.

North America lies between the Atlantic and Pacific Oceans.

South America stretches south towards the South Pole.

These globes show the seven continents

Europe is one of the smallest continents

North Pole

Pacific Ocean **NORTH AMERICA** Atlantic Ocean

Equator

North Pole

EUROPE

Equator

North Pole

SOUTH AMERICA

Equator

South Pole

North Pole

Equator

AFRICA

Equator

Africa straddles the Equator.

Latitude and longitude

We use a grid system to locate places on the Earth's surface. This was first invented by the ancient Greeks.

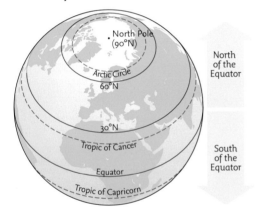

North Pole (90°N)

Arctic Circle 60°N

30°N

Tropic of Cancer

Equator

Tropic of Capricorn

North of the Equator

South of the Equator

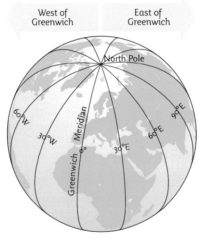

West of Greenwich   East of Greenwich

North Pole

60°W 30°W Greenwich Meridian 0° 30°E 60°E 90°E

Latitude Lines of latitude are imaginary lines which go round the Earth in hoops. They are measured in degrees north or south of the Equator.

Longitude Lines of longitude are imaginary lines which go from the North Pole to the South Pole. They are measured in degrees east or west of the Greenwich Meridian.

Activities

➤ Work out the latitude and longitude of different places around the world for a quiz.
➤ Make your own model of the world. Begin by covering a balloon with layers of papier mâché. Then paint the land and sea and add labels.
www.oxfam.org.uk/education

Which way up?

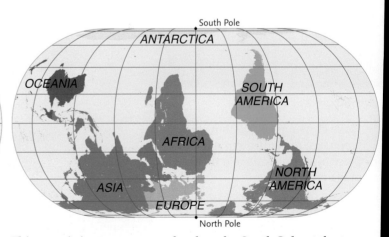

North Pole

NORTH AMERICA EUROPE ASIA

AFRICA

SOUTH AMERICA

OCEANIA

ANTARCTICA

South Pole

South Pole

ANTARCTICA

OCEANIA

SOUTH AMERICA

AFRICA

ASIA EUROPE

NORTH AMERICA

North Pole

World maps are usually drawn with the North Pole at the top. Can you find Europe?

This map is just as accurate but has the South Pole at the top. Where is Europe now?

4

Asia is the largest continent.

ASIA

North Pole

Equator

Equator

ANTARCTICA

South Pole

OCEANIA

Equator

Antarctica encircles the South Pole.

South Pole

Oceania is made up of Australia, New Zealand and many small islands.

A British mountaineer, Eric Shipton, taking measurements for a map of the Himalaya in the 1930s.

Map projections

Map makers draw the map of the world using grid systems. The maps in this atlas use a system known as Eckert IV. This shows both area and shape as accurately as possible.

Gerardus Mercator

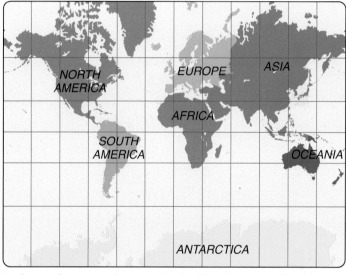

NORTH AMERICA

EUROPE

ASIA

AFRICA

SOUTH AMERICA

OCEANIA

ANTARCTICA

Tudor explorers used a map devised by Mercator. This shows compass directions accurately but distorts polar regions. For example, Greenland looks larger than South America but is really much smaller.

Historical maps of the world

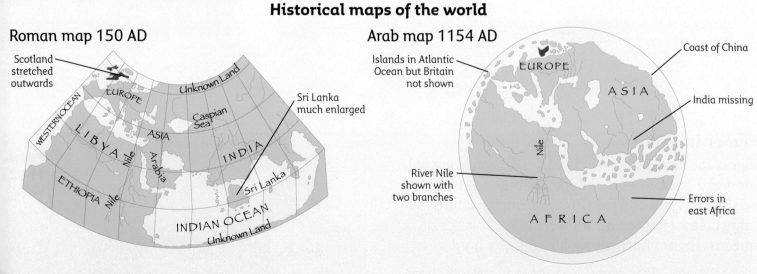

Roman map 150 AD

Scotland stretched outwards

WESTERN OCEAN

EUROPE

Unknown Land

Caspian Sea

LIBYA

Nile

ASIA

Arabia

INDIA

Sri Lanka much enlarged

ETHIOPIA

Nile

Sri Lanka

INDIAN OCEAN

Unknown Land

Arab map 1154 AD

Islands in Atlantic Ocean but Britain not shown

EUROPE

ASIA

Coast of China

India missing

Nile

River Nile shown with two branches

AFRICA

Errors in east Africa

The Greeks and the Romans knew that the Earth was a sphere. Their maps showed the places they conquered as well as countries where they traded.

This map, drawn by the Arab map maker Idrisi, shows India, China and east Africa. The Arabs traded with these places by sea.

5

World Countries

What are the countries of the world?

There are almost 200 countries in the world. They vary greatly in size. Jamaica is a small island. Canada and Russia spread over vast areas.

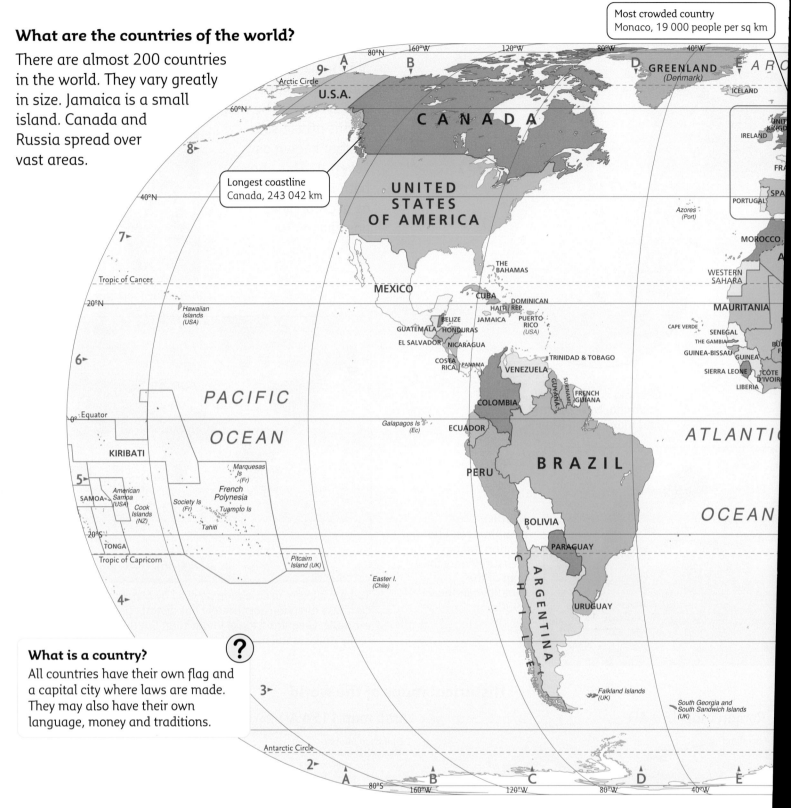

Most crowded country
Monaco, 19 000 people per sq km

Longest coastline
Canada, 243 042 km

What is a country? (?)

All countries have their own flag and a capital city where laws are made. They may also have their own language, money and traditions.

Europe in 1912

Before the First World War (1914–18) there were only around 20 countries in Europe. Germany, Russia, Austro-Hungary and the Ottoman Empire controlled large areas. Many countries were ruled by kings or queens. For ordinary people life was very hard.

Europe in 1912

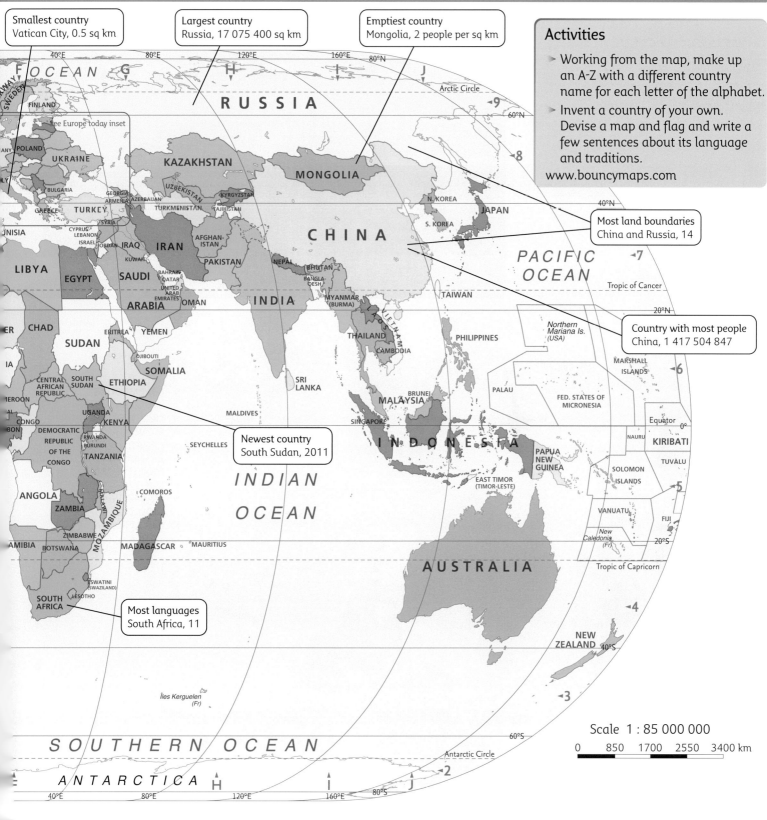

Smallest country
Vatican City, 0.5 sq km

Largest country
Russia, 17 075 400 sq km

Emptiest country
Mongolia, 2 people per sq km

Most land boundaries
China and Russia, 14

Country with most people
China, 1 417 504 847

Newest country
South Sudan, 2011

Most languages
South Africa, 11

Scale 1 : 85 000 000

0   850   1700   2550   3400 km

Activities

➤ Working from the map, make up
an A-Z with a different country
name for each letter of the alphabet.

➤ Invent a country of your own.
Devise a map and flag and write a
few sentences about its language
and traditions.

www.bouncymaps.com

Europe today

After the First World War (1914–18) the old empires
were broken up. Many new countries were created
including Finland, Poland and the Ukraine. In Russia
the communists gained power. Europe was torn apart
again in the Second World War (1939–45) but most
countries kept the same boundaries afterwards.

Europe

What is Europe like?

Europe is one of the smallest continents. There are over 40 countries with 742 million people. France and Ukraine are the largest countries. Russia is even bigger but is divided between Europe and Asia.

With a population of 11 million people, Paris is one of the largest cities in Europe.

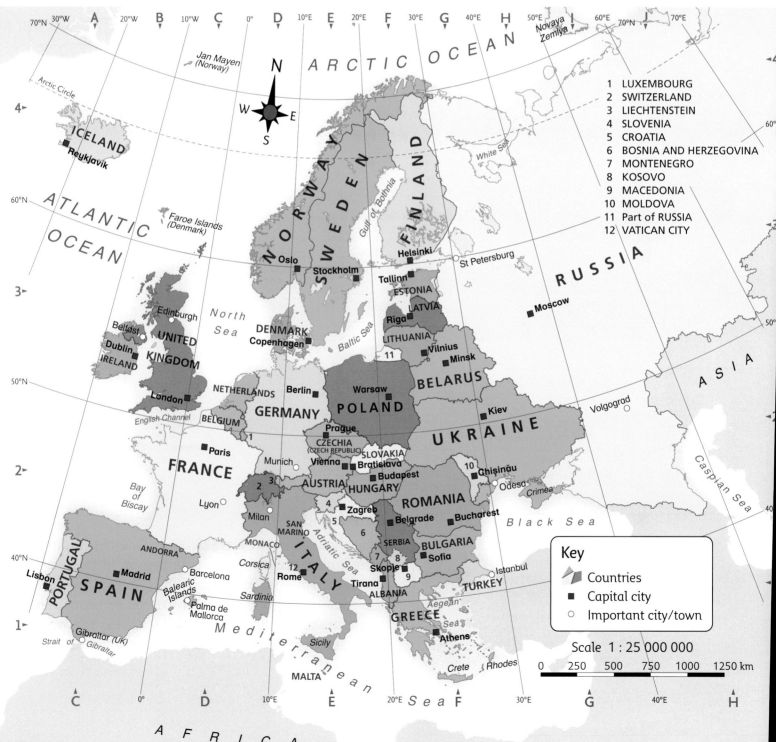

1   LUXEMBOURG
2   SWITZERLAND
3   LIECHTENSTEIN
4   SLOVENIA
5   CROATIA
6   BOSNIA AND HERZEGOVINA
7   MONTENEGRO
8   KOSOVO
9   MACEDONIA
10 MOLDOVA
11 Part of RUSSIA
12 VATICAN CITY

Key

◤ Countries
■ Capital city
○ Important city/town

Scale 1 : 25 000 000

0   250   500   750   1000   1250 km

Europe environments

Europe lies half way between the Equator and the North Pole. The Alps are one of the highest mountain ranges. These mountains are the source of two great rivers, the Rhine and the Danube. Around the coast of Europe there are many seas. One of them, the Mediterranean, is famous for its beautiful islands.

Activities

➤ What is special about Europe?
➤ Using the maps, make up a quiz with questions about Europe. Other children have to guess the answers.
www.bbc.co.uk/schools/primaryhistory/ancient_greeks/

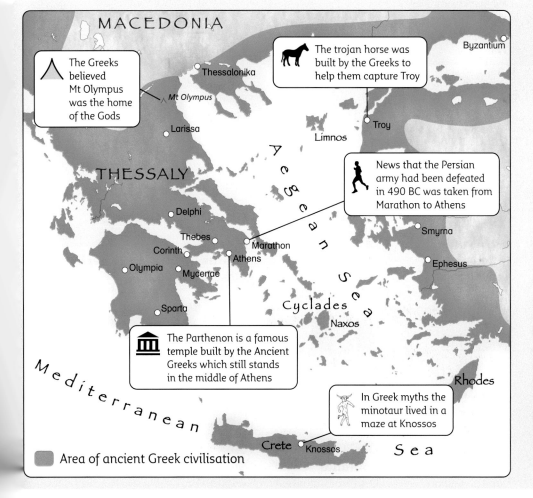

Ancient Greece

Many of the ideas that we use in art and science today go back to the ancient Greeks. This map shows the Greek Empire about 500 BC. At that time it was split into many different city states.

The ruins of the Parthenon still tower over modern Athens.

The European Union

What is the European Union?

The European Union was founded to improve living standards after the Second World War when much of Europe lay in ruins. People decided to work together to keep the peace. Today nearly 500 million people live in countries that belong to the EU.

The EU flag.

Comparing this satellite image and the map shows how closely all the different countries are linked together.

Members of the EU: This diagram shows the countries which belonged to the EU in 2018, the date when they joined and their capital city.

The European Union

 1995

Austria
Capital: Vienna

 1957

Belgium
Capital: Brussels

2007

Bulgaria
Capital: Sofia

 2013

Croatia
Capital: Zagreb

 2004

Cyprus
Capital: Nicosia

 2004

**Czechia
(Czech Republic)**
Capital: Prague

1957

Germany
Capital: Berlin

1981

Greece
Capital: Athens

 2004

Hungary
Capital: Budapest

 1973

Ireland
Capital: Dublin

 1957

Italy
Capital: Rome

 2004

Latvia
Capital: Riga

 1957

Netherlands
Capital: Amsterdam/
The Hague

2004

Poland
Capital: Warsaw

 1986

Portugal
Capital: Lisbon

 2007

Romania
Capital: Bucharest

 2004

Slovakia
Capital: Bratislava

 200

Slovenia
Capital: Ljubljan

Key

- Founder member in 1957
- Joined since 1957
- Hoping to join
- Other countries
- Voted to leave in 2016

1 LUXEMBOURG
2 SWITZERLAND
3 LIECHTENSTEIN
4 SLOVENIA
5 CROATIA
6 BOSNIA AND HERZEGOVINA
7 MONTENEGRO
8 KOSOVO
9 MACEDONIA
10 MOLDOVA
11 Part of RUSSIA

What has the EU achieved?

Trade
Traders can sell their goods in other EU countries without tax

Money
Some EU countries have the same money (the euro)

Farming
People get cheap food but farmers are properly paid

Working conditions
There are EU laws about working hours, safety and levels of pay

Human rights
The EU defends people's freedom, safety and equality

Environment
EU countries are working together to protect the environment

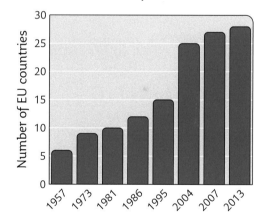

Growth of the EU

The UK and the EU
The UK was part of the European Union for over 40 years. In 2016 the UK voted to leave the EU because people wanted more independence. It is now trying to find new ways of linking with other countries.

 1973
Denmark
Capital: Copenhagen

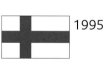 2004
Estonia
Capital: Tallinn

 1995
Finland
Capital: Helsinki

1957
France
Capital: Paris

2004
Lithuania
Capital: Vilnius

 1957
Luxembourg
Capital: Luxembourg

2004
Malta
Capital: Valletta

1986
Spain
Capital: Madrid

 1995
Sweden
Capital: Stockholm

 1973
United Kingdom
Capital: London

Activities

➤ Make up a word search containing the names of ten or more European Union countries.

➤ Make a list of the advantages and disadvantages of being part of the European Union.

europa.eu/kids-corner/index_en.htm
www.europeoftales.net/site/en

Africa

What is Africa like?

Africa is the second largest continent. Most of the northern part is covered by the Sahara desert. Further south there are grasslands, rainforests and mountains.

There are over 50 countries in Africa. The largest are Algeria, Democratic Republic of the Congo and Sudan.

The British Isles at the same scale.

Key
- ◢ Countries
- ■ Capital city
- ○ Important city/town

Scale 1 : 40 000 000

0   500   1000   1500   2000 km

Activities

➤ Estimate how many times larger you think Africa is than the UK.

➤ Make up a fact file with ten interesting facts about Africa.

www.aworldaware.org

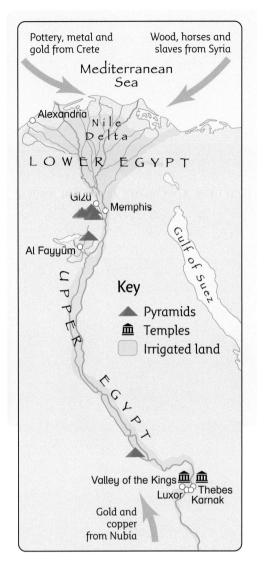

Ancient Egypt

Five thousand years ago the farmers who settled on the banks of the river Nile set up a new way of life. This became one of the world's greatest civilisations. The buildings that they put up and the objects that they made can still be seen today.

Many paintings have survived from ancient Egypt because they were on the walls of the tombs. They tell us what people believed at the time.

The pyramids at Giza were built as tombs for the pharaohs (kings). They are one of the seven wonders of the ancient world.

Colonial powers in 1914

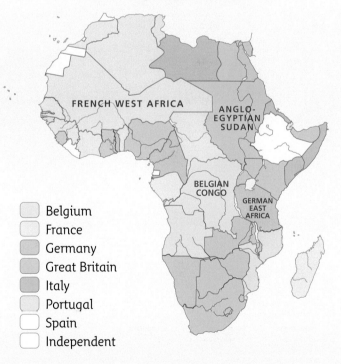

Belgium
France
Germany
Great Britain
Italy
Portugal
Spain
Independent

In Victorian times much of Africa was ruled by Europeans. Britain and France had empires that stretched across the continent. Many African countries became independent in the 1960s and 1970s. They still supply Europe and the rest of the world with food and metals at very low prices.

Africa environments

Desert
Grassland
Forest
Mediterranean
Mountain

Asia

What is Asia like?

Asia is the biggest continent. China, India and Russia are the largest countries. There are also many large cities such as Tokyo, Beijing and Mumbai.

Key

- Countries
- ■ Capital city
- ○ Important city/town

The British Isles at the same scale.

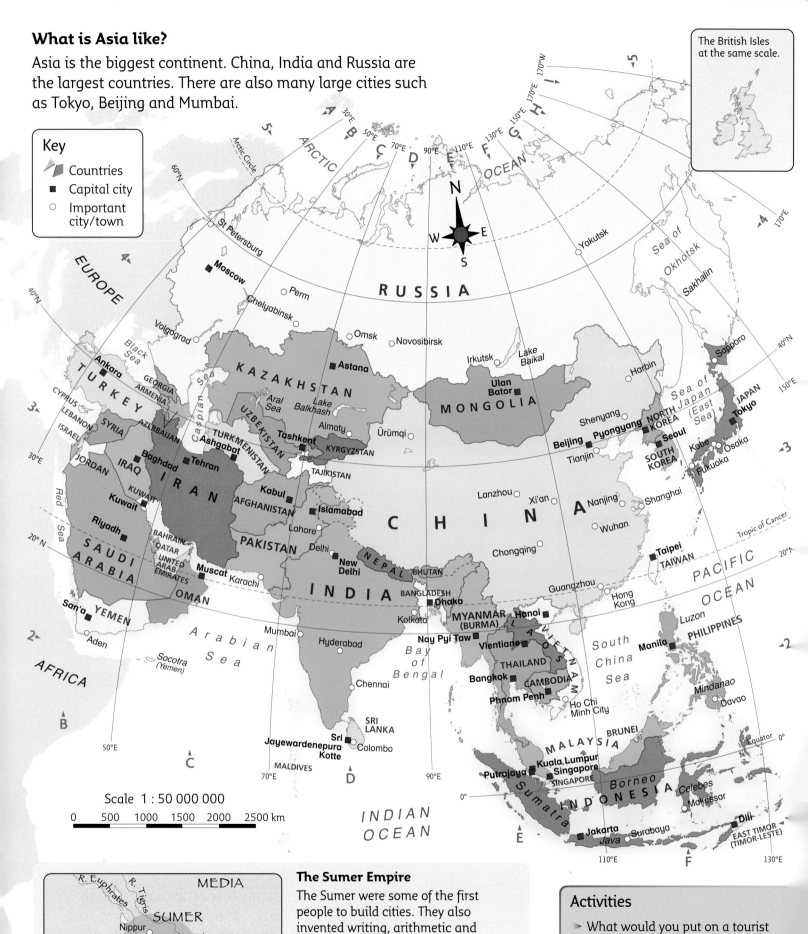

Scale 1 : 50 000 000

0   500   1000   1500   2000   2500 km

The Sumer Empire

The Sumer were some of the first people to build cities. They also invented writing, arithmetic and schools. The Sumer civilisation grew up in the valleys of the Tigris and Euphrates rivers around 6000 years ago. This area is now in Iraq.

Sumer area

Activities

- ➤ What would you put on a tourist website about Asia?
- ➤ Make up a word search using the names of Asian countries.

www.oxfam.org.uk/education

14

Asia environments

ARCTIC OCEAN

Sea of Okhotsk

Ural Mountains

Black Sea

Caspian Sea

R. Euphrates

R. Tigris

Altai Mountains

Lake Baikal

Tien Shan

Gobi Desert

Huang He

Arabian Peninsula

K2

R. Indus

Himalaya

Mount Everest

R. Ganges

Chang Jiang

PACIFIC OCEAN

Arabian Sea

Bay of Bengal

South China Sea

INDIAN OCEAN

- Ice cap
- Tundra
- Desert
- Grassland
- Forest
- Mediterranean
- ∧ Mountain

Asia is the largest continent. It has many of the world's highest mountains and longest rivers. The peaks of the Himalaya stretch for 3000 km across central Asia. From here, water flows down the Indus, Ganges, Chang Jiang and other rivers to the sea.

This remarkable landscape in southern China attracts millions of tourists every year.

The Indus Valley

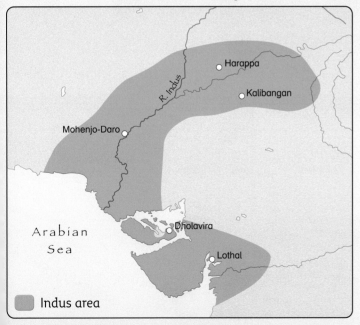

Harappa

Kalibangan

R. Indus

Mohenjo-Daro

Dholavira

Lothal

Arabian Sea

- Indus area

About 5000 years ago the Indus Valley was the centre of a great civilisation. Cities that depended on trade were established on the river banks. The beliefs that date from this time are still found in India and Pakistan today.

Ancient China

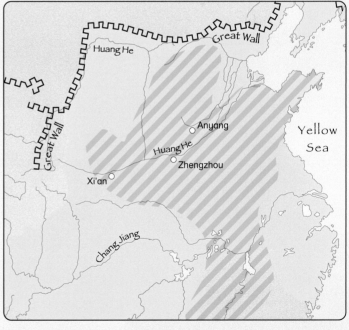

Great Wall

Huang He

Great Wall

Anyang

Huang He

Zhengzhou

Xi'an

Chang Jiang

Yellow Sea

- Ch'in Empire (221–206 BC)
- Shang Empire (around 1600–1150 BC)

The Shangs started to unite China but it was the Ch'ins who first made it a single country. They built the Great Wall to keep out invaders from the north. Their leaders were buried with a massive army of clay soldiers (the terracotta army) which was only discovered in the 1970s.

North America

What is North America like?

Canada, the USA and Mexico are the three largest countries in North America.
There are many small countries around the shores of the Caribbean Sea.

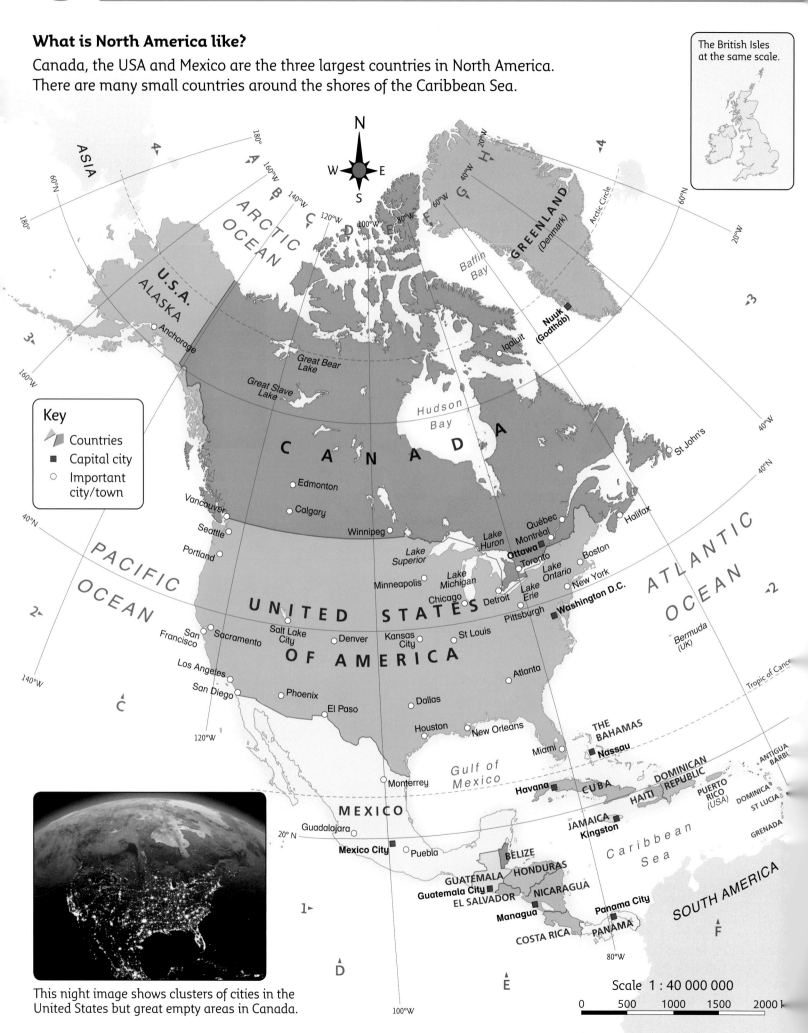

The British Isles at the same scale.

Key

- ◢ Countries
- ■ Capital city
- ○ Important city/town

ASIA

ARCTIC OCEAN

U.S.A.
ALASKA
Anchorage

GREENLAND
(Denmark)

Baffin Bay

Nuuk (Godthåb)

Iqaluit

Great Bear Lake

Great Slave Lake

Hudson Bay

C A N A D A

St John's

Edmonton

Calgary

Vancouver

Seattle

Portland

Winnipeg

Lake Superior

Lake Huron

Québec

Montréal

Ottawa

Toronto

Lake Ontario

Lake Erie

Halifax

Boston

New York

ATLANTIC OCEAN

PACIFIC OCEAN

Minneapolis

Lake Michigan

Chicago

Detroit

Pittsburgh

Washington D.C.

San Francisco

Sacramento

Salt Lake City

Denver

Kansas City

St Louis

UNITED STATES OF AMERICA

Los Angeles

San Diego

Phoenix

El Paso

Dallas

Atlanta

Bermuda (UK)

Houston

New Orleans

Tropic of Cancer

Monterrey

Gulf of Mexico

Miami

THE BAHAMAS

Nassau

MEXICO

Guadalajara

Havana

CUBA

DOMINICAN REPUBLIC

HAITI

PUERTO RICO (USA)

ANTIGUA & BARB...

DOMINICA

ST LUCIA

Caribbean Sea

GRENADA

Mexico City

Puebla

JAMAICA

Kingston

BELIZE

GUATEMALA

HONDURAS

Guatemala City

EL SALVADOR

NICARAGUA

Panama City

SOUTH AMERICA

Managua

COSTA RICA

PANAMA

This night image shows clusters of cities in the United States but great empty areas in Canada.

Scale 1 : 40 000 000

0   500   1000   1500   2000 k

North America environments

ARCTIC OCEAN

Greenland

Denali

Mount Logan

Rocky Mountains

Hudson Bay

PACIFIC OCEAN

Great Lakes

R. Mississippi

ATLANTIC OCEAN

Grand Canyon

Gulf of Mexico

Popocatépetl

Caribbean Sea

- Ice cap
- Tundra
- Desert
- Grassland
- Forest
- Mediterranean
- ∧ Mountain

The Rocky Mountains stretch down the western side of North America. To the east there are lakes and plains. In the north, Greenland is covered by ice.

Activities

➤ Which North American countries are islands?
➤ Imagine you are writing a postcard to a friend about North America. What three things would you say about (a) the countries (b) the mountains, seas and rivers?
www.ducksters.com/geography/northamerica.php

European settlement before 1763

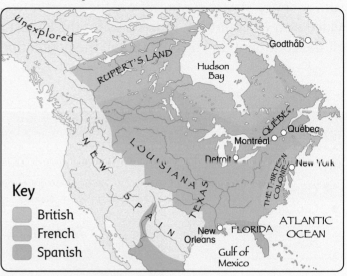

Unexplored

Godthåb

RUPERT'S LAND

Hudson Bay

NEW

QUÉBEC

Québec

Montréal

Detroit

LOUISIANA

New York

SPAIN

THE THIRTEEN COLONIES

TEXAS

FLORIDA

ATLANTIC OCEAN

New Orleans

Gulf of Mexico

Key
- British
- French
- Spanish

The American Indians and Inuit have lived in North America for thousands of years. In the last 400 years people from Europe and Asia have also made it their home. At the same time, thousands of Africans were brought as slaves to work in the sugar plantations and cotton fields.

The Pilgrim Fathers left England for America in 1620 on the Mayflower. This painting was made afterwards.

Lake Texcoco Tenochtitlán

Gulf of Mexico

Chichén Itzá

Mayapán

Yucatán Peninsula

Gulf of Honduras

Key
- Maya Empire (around 900)
- Aztec Empire (around 1500)

Maya Empire

The Maya built great palaces and learned about the stars. They also discovered the importance of using a nought (or zero) in mathematics. Their empire was at its peak at the time when the Vikings were invading Britain.

Aztec Empire

The Aztec Empire dates from Tudor times. They were clever farmers and fierce fighters. They also believed in many gods.

17

South America

What is South America like?

South America stretches south from the Equator towards Antarctica. It is divided into 13 countries. Brazil is by far the largest country. It covers about half the continent and has about half the population.

The British Isles at the same scale.

Key
- Countries
- ■ Capital city
- ○ Important city/town

NORTH AMERICA

Caribbean Sea

Barranquilla Maracaibo Caracas Port of Spain TRINIDAD AND TOBAGO

VENEZUELA

Medellín Georgetown Paramaribo Cayenne GUYANA SURINAME FRENCH GUIANA

Bogotá COLOMBIA

Cali

Quito ECUADOR Equator

Galapagos Islands (Ecuador) Guayaquil Belém São Luís Fortaleza

Iquitos Manaus Natal

B R A Z I L

Trujillo Recife

PERU Aracaju

Lima Salvador

PACIFIC OCEAN

Lake Titicaca BOLIVIA Brasília

Arequipa La Paz

Sucre Belo Horizonte

Antofagasta PARAGUAY São Paulo Rio de Janeiro

Asunción Curitiba ATLANTIC OCEAN

Tropic of Capricorn

Valparaíso URUGUAY Porto Alegre

Santiago Buenos Aires Montevideo

Concepción ARGENTINA Mar del Plata

Scale 1 : 40 000 000
0   500   1000   1500   2000 kr

Falkland Islands (UK)

Punta Arenas Tierra del Fuego

South Georgia (UK)

South Orkney Islands (UK)

In this satellite image the Amazon rainforests are deep green. Patches of cloud are shown in white.

Activities

- Why do you think Chile is so long and thin? What other countries around the world have a similar shape?
- Draw your own map of South America. Name six features and write a sentence about each one.

www.andes.org

South America environments

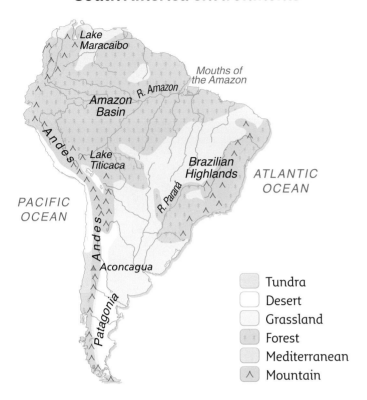

Key:
- Tundra
- Desert
- Grassland
- Forest
- Mediterranean
- ∧ Mountain

The Andes mountains run right down the western edge of South America. They form the longest mountain range in the world. The river Amazon rises in the Andes and flows east through rainforests to the Atlantic Ocean.

European settlement in 1650

Key
- Spain
- Portugal
- France
- Great Britain
- Netherlands
- Unsettled

As they explored the world, the Spanish and Portuguese came to South America looking for gold and silver. The Portuguese settled in the east which is why Portuguese is spoken in Brazil today. The Spanish settled in the other parts of the continent so Spanish is the main language everywhere else.

The Inca Empire

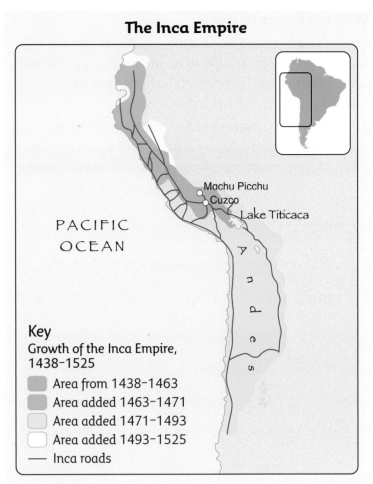

Key
Growth of the Inca Empire, 1438–1525
- Area from 1438–1463
- Area added 1463–1471
- Area added 1471–1493
- Area added 1493–1525
- —— Inca roads

In Tudor times the Inca Empire stretched along the Andes. Places were linked by a vast network of roads. A few hundred Spanish soldiers were able to conquer the Inca because they had no guns, horses or armour.

The ruins of the lost Inca city of Machu Picchu were discovered high in the Andes a hundred years ago.

Oceania and the Pacific Islands

What is Oceania like?

Oceania is the smallest continent. Australia is the main land mass. Groups of islands make up the rest of the continent. These stretch thousands of kilometres across the Pacific Ocean.

Although it is surrounded by water, Australia is famous for deserts. New Zealand and New Guinea have high mountains. Many of the islands are made of coral or old volcanoes which have worn away.

Activities

▷ List the things that make Oceania different from other continents.

▷ Make up a map of an imaginary island. Do drawings of the coast, plants and creatures.

www.cia.gov/library/publications/the-world-factbook

Oceania environments

Key:
- ☐ Desert
- ☐ Grassland
- ☐ Forest
- ☐ Mediterranean
- ⋀ Mountain

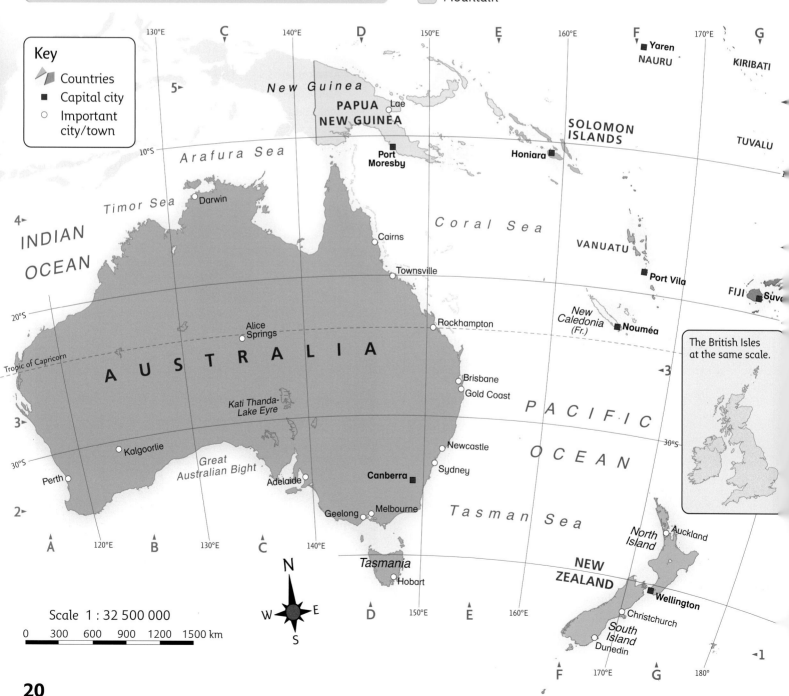

Key
- Countries
- ■ Capital city
- ○ Important city/town

Scale 1 : 32 500 000

0   300   600   900   1200   1500 km

The British Isles at the same scale.

European settlers in Australia

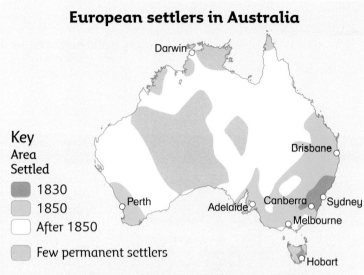

Key
Area
Settled

- 1830
- 1850
- After 1850
- Few permanent settlers

Europeans first settled around Sydney. They moved inland in Victorian times. Some were farmers. Others were looking for gold. As they spread, the space left for native people (aborigines) became less and less.

Cook's first voyage, 1768–71

In 1768 Captain Cook set off to the South Seas to search for an unknown continent. He became the first person to sail round New Zealand. He also landed near Sydney in eastern Australia, claiming it for Britain.

Pacific islands

There are 20 to 30 thousand islands in the Pacific Ocean. Volcanoes form high islands. Coral reefs are low and only rise just above sea level.

Clouds hang over the mountains of Fiji in the middle of the Pacific Ocean.

Fiji

Fiji is formed from old volcanoes. The summits are over 1000 metres high. This map shows the two largest islands.

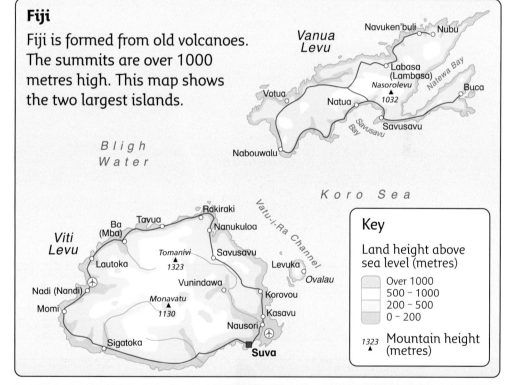

Key

Land height above sea level (metres)

- Over 1000
- 500 – 1000
- 200 – 500
- 0 – 200

1323 ▲ Mountain height (metres)

Tuvalu is a country of nine low coral reefs, north of Fiji. It could be threatened if sea levels rise.

21

The Arctic Ocean

What is the Arctic Ocean like?

The Arctic Ocean is the smallest ocean in the world. In winter it is very cold and the sea is covered in ice. In the summer whales, seals and other creatures come to the Arctic Ocean looking for food as the ice melts.

Scale 1 : 35 000 000

0   500   1000   1500   2000 km

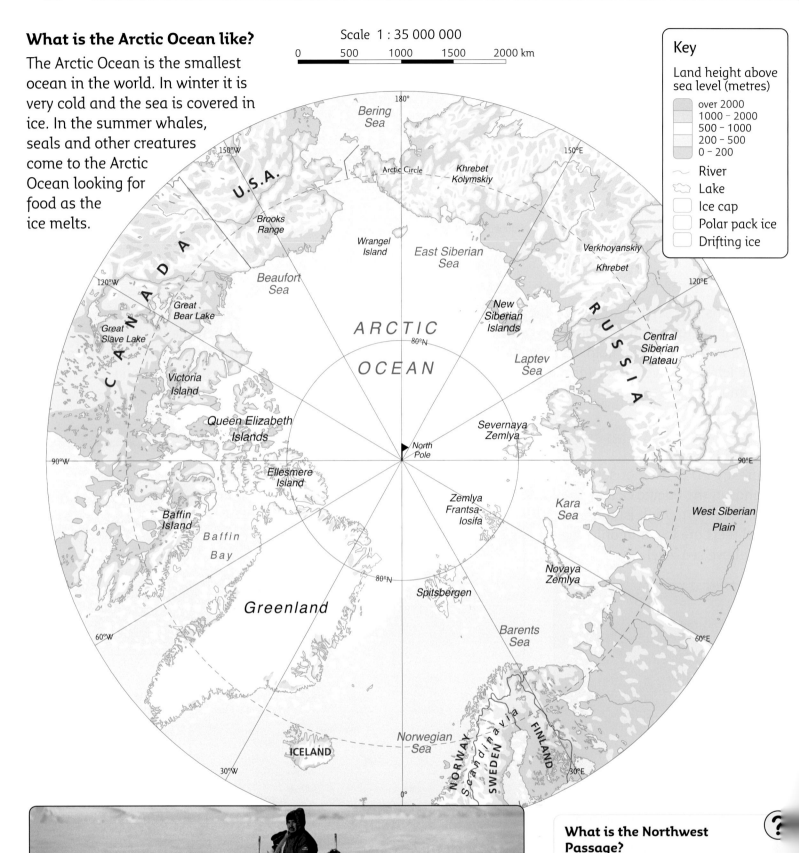

The people who live in the Arctic are known as the Inuit.

What is the Northwest Passage?

The shortest sea route between the Atlantic and Pacific Oceans goes round northern Canada. This was known as the Northwest Passage. In the past, explorers found that the route was blocked by ice all year round. Now the ice has started to melt so ships can go there. Scientists think this is due to global warming.

What is Antarctica like?

Antarctica is the world's coldest, driest and windiest continent. It is covered by a sheet of ice. In places the ice is thicker than the height of any mountain in the UK. Very few plants and animals can survive here.

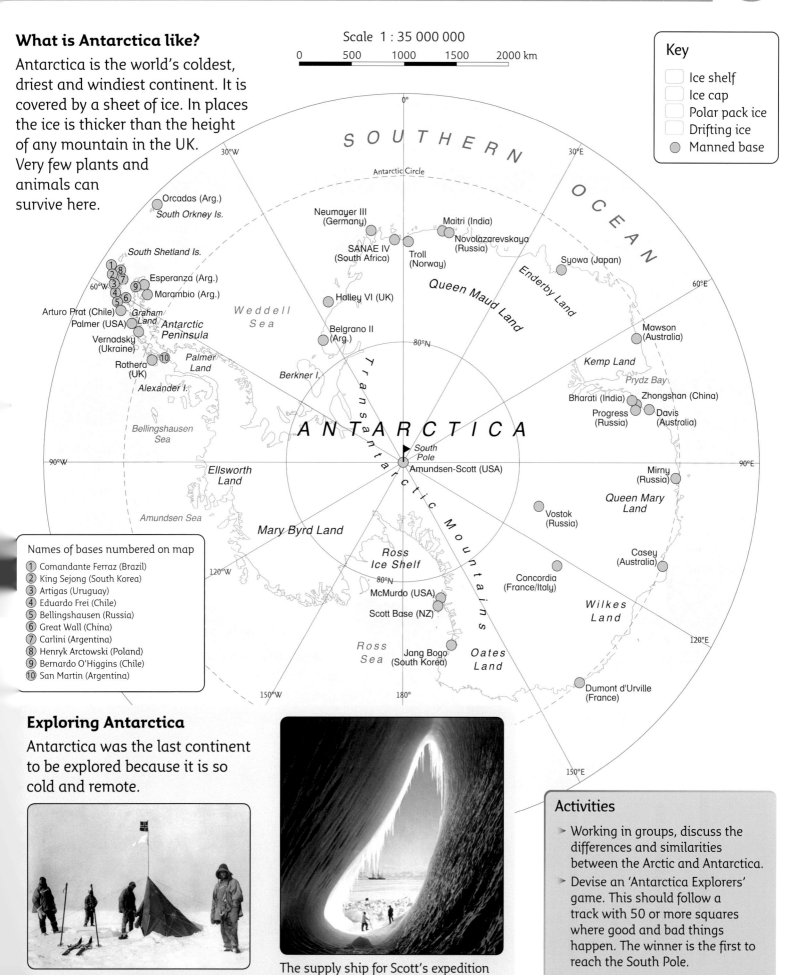

Scale 1 : 35 000 000

0   500   1000   1500   2000 km

Key
- Ice shelf
- Ice cap
- Polar pack ice
- Drifting ice
- Manned base

SOUTHERN OCEAN

Antarctic Circle

Orcadas (Arg.)
South Orkney Is.

South Shetland Is.

Neumayer III (Germany)

Maitri (India)
Novolazarevskaya (Russia)

SANAE IV (South Africa)
Troll (Norway)

Syowa (Japan)

Enderby Land

Esperanza (Arg.)
Marambio (Arg.)

Queen Maud Land

Halley VI (UK)

Weddell Sea

Arturo Prat (Chile)
Palmer (USA)
Graham Land
Antarctic Peninsula

Belgrano II (Arg.)

Mawson (Australia)

Vernadsky (Ukraine)
Rothera (UK)

Berkner I.

Kemp Land

Prydz Bay

Alexander I.

Bharati (India)
Zhongshan (China)
Progress (Russia)
Davis (Australia)

Bellingshausen Sea

ANTARCTICA

Ellsworth Land

South Pole
Amundsen-Scott (USA)

Mirny (Russia)

Amundsen Sea

Queen Mary Land

Mary Byrd Land

Vostok (Russia)

Casey (Australia)

Ross Ice Shelf

Concordia (France/Italy)

Wilkes Land

McMurdo (USA)
Scott Base (NZ)

Ross Sea

Jang Bogo (South Korea)

Oates Land

Dumont d'Urville (France)

Names of bases numbered on map
1. Comandante Ferraz (Brazil)
2. King Sejong (South Korea)
3. Artigas (Uruguay)
4. Eduardo Frei (Chile)
5. Bellingshausen (Russia)
6. Great Wall (China)
7. Carlini (Argentina)
8. Henryk Arctowski (Poland)
9. Bernardo O'Higgins (Chile)
10. San Martin (Argentina)

Exploring Antarctica

Antarctica was the last continent to be explored because it is so cold and remote.

Captain Scott and his team at the South Pole in 1912.

The supply ship for Scott's expedition (the *Terra Nova*), seen from an ice grotto.

Activities

- Working in groups, discuss the differences and similarities between the Arctic and Antarctica.
- Devise an 'Antarctica Explorers' game. This should follow a track with 50 or more squares where good and bad things happen. The winner is the first to reach the South Pole.

http://images.rgs.org
www.southpolestation.com

People and Cities

Where do most people live?

People are spread unevenly across the Earth's surface. Some of the most crowded areas are Europe, India, China, Japan and the United States. Food and crops grow well here. Other parts are much emptier. One reason is that harsh climates make living difficult.

World population

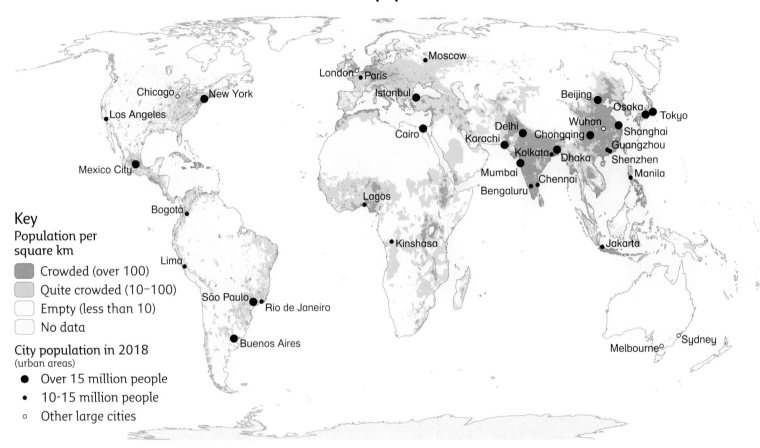

Key

Population per square km

- Crowded (over 100)
- Quite crowded (10–100)
- Empty (less than 10)
- No data

City population in 2018 (urban areas)

- ● Over 15 million people
- • 10-15 million people
- ○ Other large cities

City populations
(urban areas)

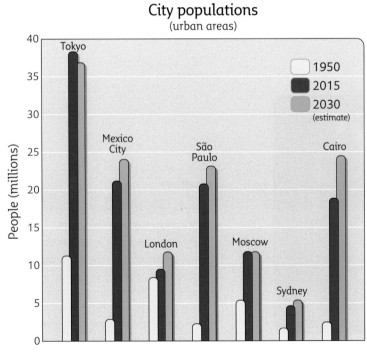

- 1950
- 2015
- 2030 (estimate)

Many cities have more than doubled in size since 1950. They are expected to go on growing.

People on the move

People move to cities for many reasons. They are attracted by the jobs and a more exciting life. They are driven from their homes by poverty and disasters.

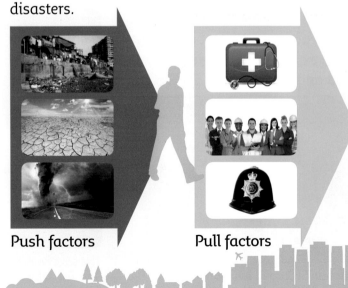

Push factors   Pull factors

Population comparisons

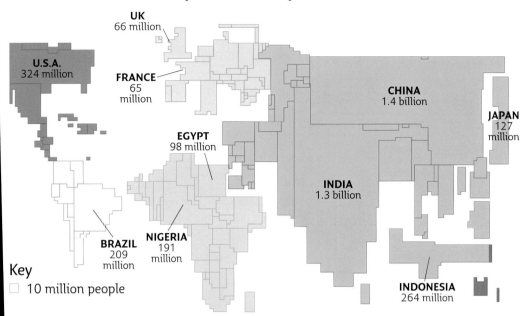

UK 66 million

U.S.A. 324 million

FRANCE 65 million

CHINA 1.4 billion

JAPAN 127 million

EGYPT 98 million

INDIA 1.3 billion

NIGERIA 191 million

BRAZIL 209 million

INDONESIA 264 million

Key
☐ 10 million people

In this diagram the size of the country matches the number of people who live there. This helps you to make comparisons. China and India have the largest populations. A different colour has been used for each continent.

Activities

> Make a list of cities with
> (a) over 15 million people
> (b) 10–15 million people.
> Is there a limit to the number of people the Earth can cope with?

www.populationmatters.org/

The fumes from traffic are one of the disadvantages of city life.

Throughout history more people have lived in the country than in towns. This has now changed. As cities keep growing, the majority of people now live in built up areas.

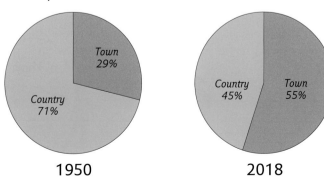

Town 29%

Country 71%

1950

Country 45%

Town 55%

2018

World cities

In 1900 only a few cities had a population over a million. London, Paris and New York were three of them. Today there are hundreds of cities this size all over the world. China and India have the most.

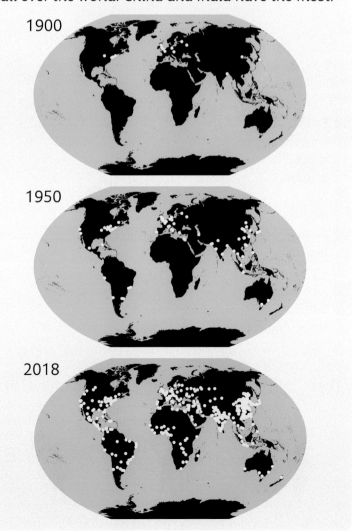

1900

1950

2018

Language

What are the different languages of the world?

There is an amazing variety of languages in the world today. Each language expresses the values and beliefs of the people who speak it. It also tends to reflect the place or region where it developed.

How many languages are there? ?

There are 7105 living languages in the world today. Mandarin (Chinese) is spoken by more people than any other language. English is the most widely used; it spread first with the British Empire and then with American influence.

Activities

➤ Make a survey of the languages people speak in your class and school.

http://aboutworldlanguages.com

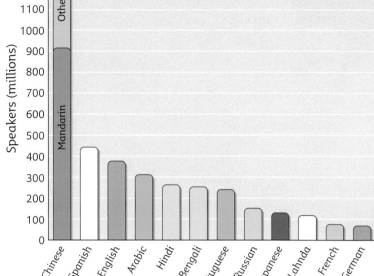

World languages
(native speakers)

World languages

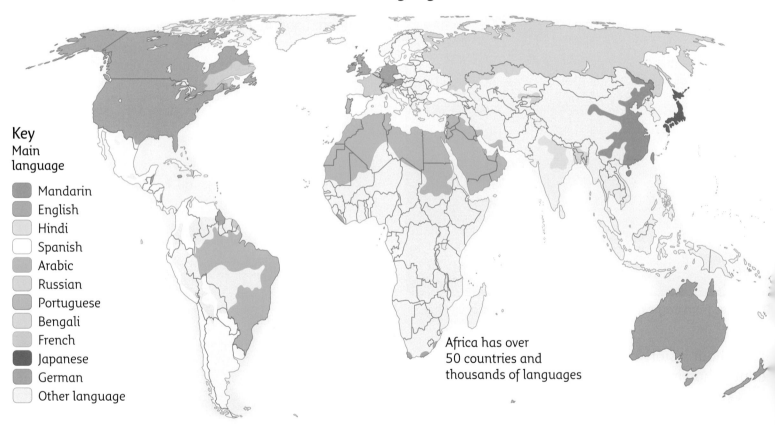

Key
Main language

- Mandarin
- English
- Hindi
- Spanish
- Arabic
- Russian
- Portuguese
- Bengali
- French
- Japanese
- German
- Other language

Africa has over 50 countries and thousands of languages

These children are each saying "Good morning" in their own language.

Good morning	Bonjour	Buenos días	Shubha prabhaat	Ni zao	Sabaah al-khayr
English	French	Spanish	Hindi	Mandarin	Arabic

What are the different religions of the world?

Some religions, like Christianity and Islam, are spread widely across the world. Others, like Hinduism, are limited to certain areas. This map shows the main religion in each country. However, in many places there is a mixture of communities of different faiths.

Activities

➤ As a research activity, find out about what is special about the places labelled on the map.
www.primaryhomeworkhelp.co.uk/Religion.html

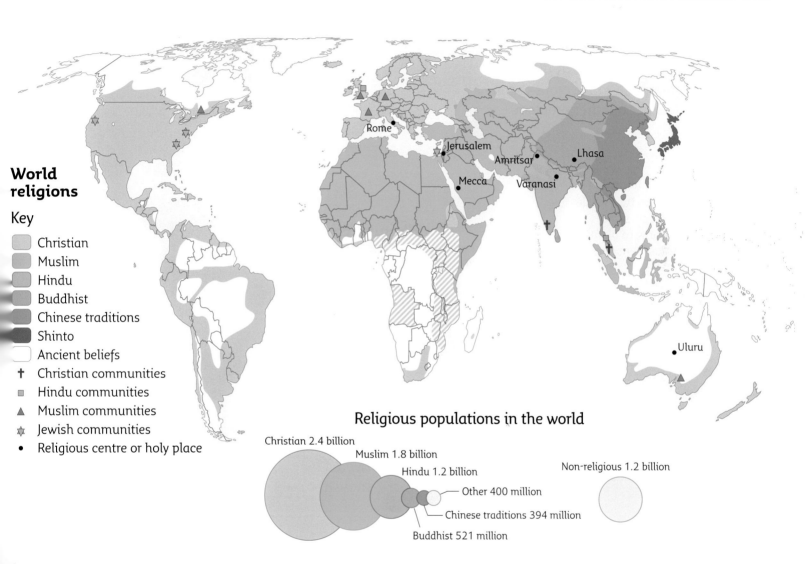

World religions

Key

- Christian
- Muslim
- Hindu
- Buddhist
- Chinese traditions
- Shinto
- Ancient beliefs
- † Christian communities
- ▪ Hindu communities
- ▲ Muslim communities
- ✡ Jewish communities
- • Religious centre or holy place

Map labels: Rome, Jerusalem, Amritsar, Lhasa, Mecca, Varanasi, Uluru

Religious populations in the world

- Christian 2.4 billion
- Muslim 1.8 billion
- Hindu 1.2 billion
- Other 400 million
- Chinese traditions 394 million
- Buddhist 521 million
- Non-religious 1.2 billion

Jerusalem is one of the oldest cities in the world. It is the spiritual centre for Jewish people and a holy city for both Christians and Muslims.

Every year over two million Muslims go on a pilgrimage (hajj) to Mecca. The Kaaba, the huge black stone in the centre of this photograph, is the most holy place in Islam.

🌐 Food and Farming

Where does our food come from?

Farmers grow the food we eat. Some farms are very small and just provide enough food for a single family. Other farms are much larger. These are run as a business and sell crops and animals for a profit.

There is enough food in the world for everyone. However, some people go hungry every day because they can't afford to buy what they need. Also, floods, storms or very dry weather sometimes cause crops to fail. War and conflicts are another problem.

When did farming begin? ❓

Farming first began in the Middle East about 10 000 years ago. Once people had learnt how to plant crops, the first civilisations were able to develop.

Activities

- Make a survey of the food you eat in a day.
- Make a class display with symbols on a world map showing where different foods first started.

www.ciwf.org.uk/

www.oxfam.org.uk/what-we-do/
issues-we-work-on/food

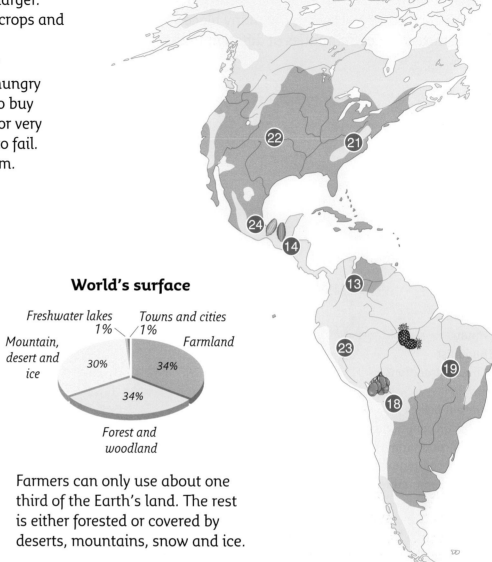

World's surface

Freshwater lakes 1%
Towns and cities 1%
Mountain, desert and ice 30%
Farmland 34%
34%

Forest and woodland

Farmers can only use about one third of the Earth's land. The rest is either forested or covered by deserts, mountains, snow and ice.

These photographs show the food eaten in a week by families in different parts of the world. Why do you think there is such a big difference?

A family in Chad, northern Africa.

A family in the USA, North America.

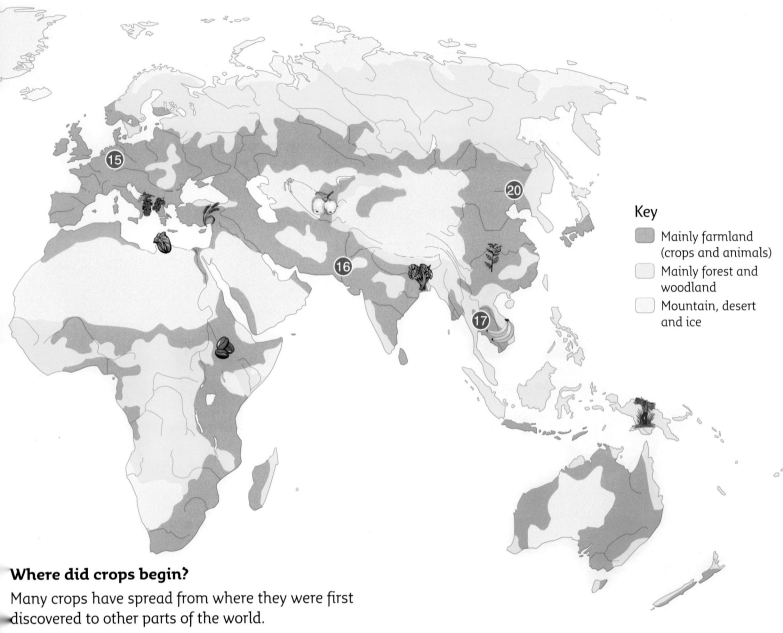

Key
- Mainly farmland (crops and animals)
- Mainly forest and woodland
- Mountain, desert and ice

Where did crops begin?

Many crops have spread from where they were first discovered to other parts of the world.

Key		Origin of crops	
1	Apples	Mountains of central Asia	Apples were grown by the first civilisations and are part of their myths.
2	Bananas	Southeast Asia	Bananas are one of the most valuable crops imported into the UK.
3	Cacao	Jungles of central America	Cacao beans are made into chocolate and were first grown by the Aztecs and Maya.
4	Coffee	Hills of east Africa	Coffee was discovered by shepherds when sheep that had eaten the beans could not sleep.
5	Grapes	Southeast Europe	Grapes were one of the first crops grown by people in ancient times.
6	Lettuce	Shores of the Mediterranean Sea	Lettuces were popular with both the Romans and the ancient Egyptians.
7	Pineapples	Jungles of South America	Christopher Columbus was the first European to taste a pineapple.
8	Potatoes	Andes mountains	Potatoes were brought to Europe by the Spanish around 1550.
9	Rice	India and southeast Asia	Rice is the main food for half the people in the world.
10	Sugar cane	South Pacific islands	Sugar was taken to America by Arab and Spanish traders.
11	Tea	China	By the end of Tudor times, tea had become Britain's national drink.
12	Wheat	River valleys in Middle East	Wheat is now grown in every continent apart from Antarctica.

Other crops
- 13 Cotton
- 14 Maize
- 15 Oats
- 16 Onions
- 17 Oranges
- 18 Peanuts
- 19 Rubber
- 20 Soybeans
- 21 Strawberries
- 22 Sunflowers
- 23 Tobacco
- 24 Tomatoes

⊕ Resources

Where do resources come from?

The Earth's surface is made of many different kinds of rock. Some of these contain the ores which can be made into metal. Others provide fuels such as coal, oil and gas.

Oil wells In Victorian times more than half the world's oil came from Azerbaijan. Today this area is still an important source of oil.

Gold mines Gold is Ghana's biggest export but there are worries that the mines are polluting streams and rivers.

Water supply

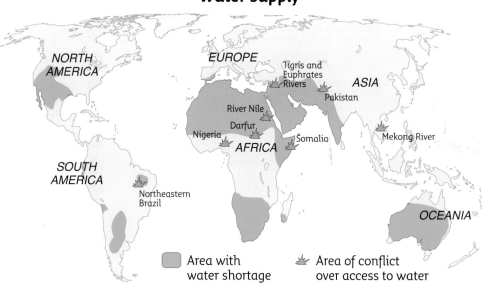

Area with water shortage

Area of conflict over access to water

Water is one of the world's most important resources. We need it for drinking, washing, cooking and cleaning. Factories use water to make goods. Crops die without rain. Water from reservoirs drives turbines to make electricity.

We are using more and more water as human numbers increase and new factories are built. In some places there are now water conflicts.

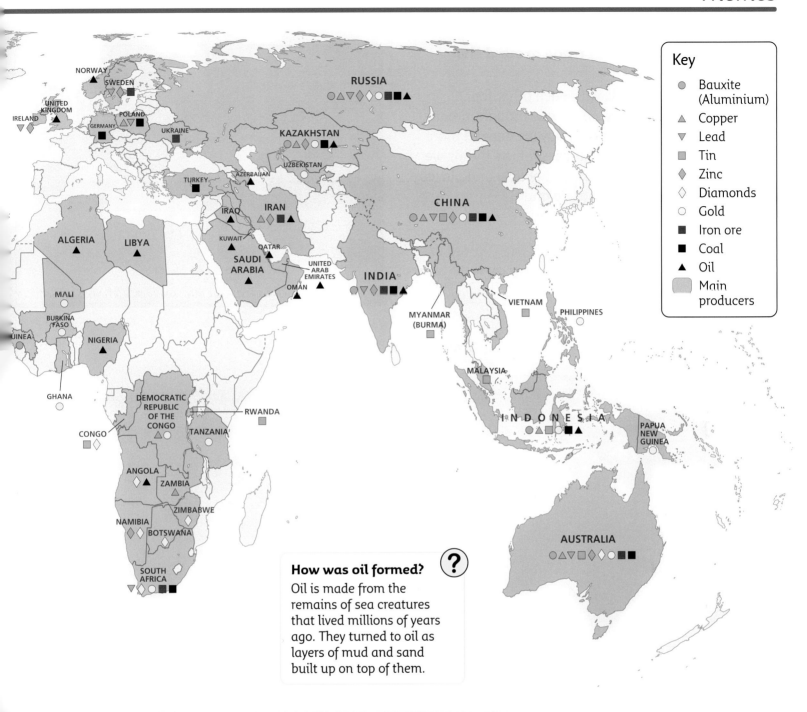

Key

- ● Bauxite (Aluminium)
- △ Copper
- ▽ Lead
- ▣ Tin
- ◇ Zinc
- ◇ Diamonds
- ○ Gold
- ■ Iron ore
- ■ Coal
- ▲ Oil
- ▨ Main producers

How was oil formed? ⑦

Oil is made from the remains of sea creatures that lived millions of years ago. They turned to oil as layers of mud and sand built up on top of them.

How long will they last?

The diagram shows how long the resources we know about will last if we go on using them as we are today. What do you think we can do to stop them running out?

Zinc	17 years
Tin	17 years
Gold	18 years
Lead	19 years
Silver	20 years
Copper	40 years
Uranium	75 years
Aluminium	1000 years or more

Recycling

Old aluminium cans can be saved and used again. The same amount of energy makes twenty recycled cans or one new one.

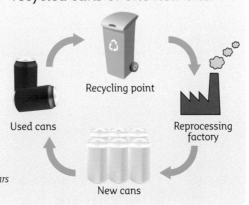

Used cans

Recycling point

Reprocessing factory

New cans

Making a difference

There are three things we can do to help save the world's resources.

- ➤ Reduce the amount we use
- ➤ Repair things when they wear out
- ➤ Recycle the materials to make something new

Activities

- ➤ Which countries on the map have five or more resources?
- ➤ Make up a poster or IT presentation to persuade children of your age to save resources.

www.recyclezone.org.uk

31

Trade

What are the patterns of trade around the world?

People have traded goods with each other for thousands of years. In the past trade brought great wealth to cities and empires. Today we depend more than ever before on other countries for the things we use in our daily lives. The way that people and places are linked together through trade and communications is called globalisation.

Some of the shops in the centre of Shanghai, China, are run by companies that trade all over the world.

Share of world trade

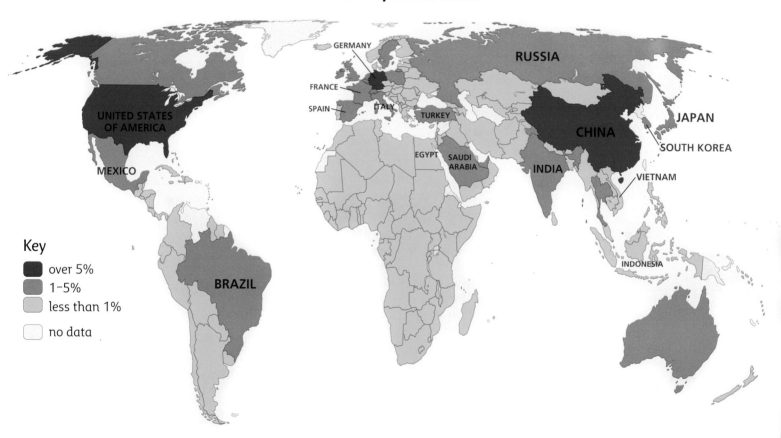

Key
- over 5%
- 1–5%
- less than 1%
- no data

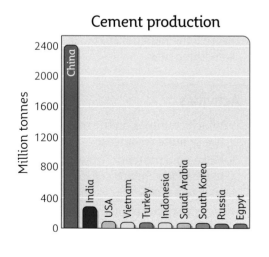

Cement production

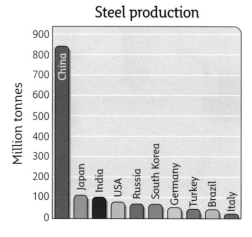

Steel production

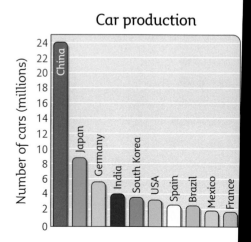

Car production

Fair trade

The price of crops and natural resources is always changing. Fair trade agreements give workers a fair wage and help to protect the environment. However fair trade goods cost more to buy and farmers who are left out of fair trade deals can find their lives become even harder.

Price of goods

This chart shows how the price of goods changes on the open market. Fair trade prices are always higher.

Where does the money go?

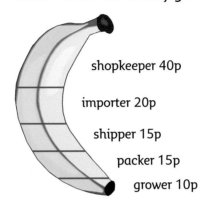

shopkeeper 40p

importer 20p

shipper 15p

packer 15p

grower 10p

This diagram shows where the money goes when you spend £1 on bananas. Only about 10p goes to the grower.

Picking bananas on a fair trade farm.

Atlantic slave trade, 1600 – 1800

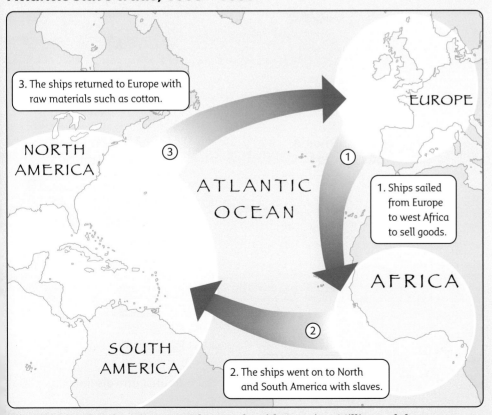

3. The ships returned to Europe with raw materials such as cotton.

NORTH AMERICA

③

ATLANTIC OCEAN

EUROPE

①

1. Ships sailed from Europe to west Africa to sell goods.

AFRICA

②

SOUTH AMERICA

2. The ships went on to North and South America with slaves.

The voyages of exploration opened up trade with America. Millions of slaves were taken across the Atlantic in this inhuman traffic.

Why do we need to trade? (?)

Many of the resources we need are distributed unevenly across the world. Also crops will only grow in places where they get the climate and soil they need. This means people have to exchange things.

Activities

➤ Make a list of all the goods from other countries that you can find in your classroom.

➤ Find out what fair trade products you can buy in local shops.

www.oxfam.org.uk/education

Air Travel

How are places around the world linked together by planes?

Air transport is the quickest way of reaching places that are far away. The main routes are in Europe and North America.

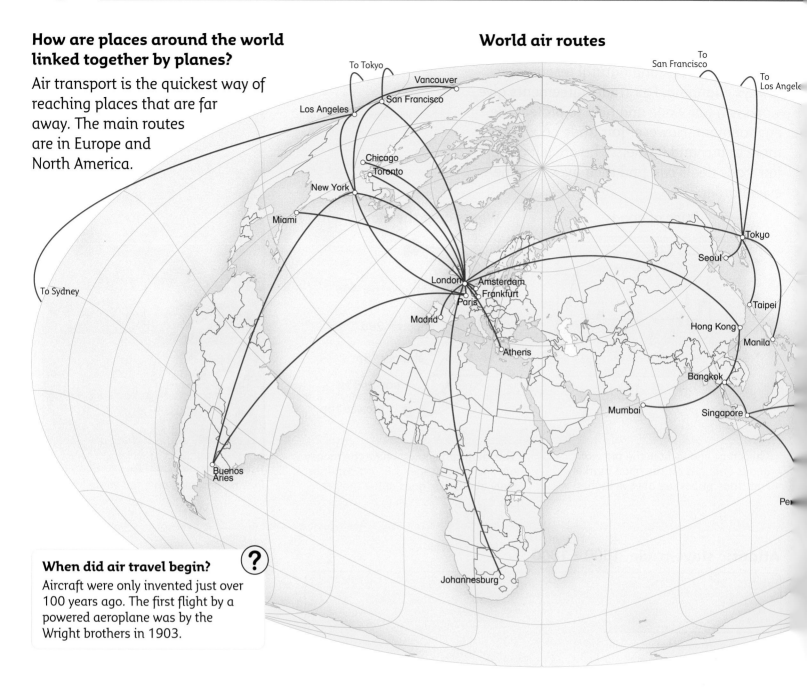

World air routes

When did air travel begin? (?)

Aircraft were only invented just over 100 years ago. The first flight by a powered aeroplane was by the Wright brothers in 1903.

Top ten airports by passengers

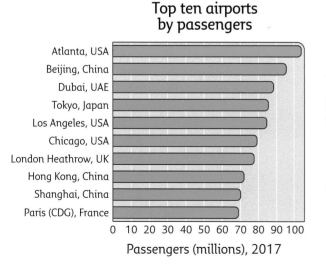

Passengers (millions), 2017

The world's busiest airport is in the USA. It has more passengers each year than the entire UK population.

Total worldwide passengers

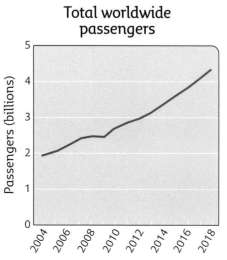

Air travel is one of the cheapest ways to travel. The demand goes on growing from year to year.

Top ten tourist destinations

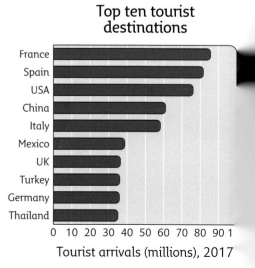

Tourist arrivals (millions), 2017

People travel by plane for their wor and holidays. France and Spain are the two most popular destinations

Flight times between major cities

From	To	Journey time (hours)
London	Johannesburg	11
London	New York	7½
Los Angeles	Tokyo	11½
New York	Buenos Aires	11
Paris	Buenos Aires	13
Singapore	Sydney	8

Activities

➤ What are the advantages and disadvantages of air travel?
➤ Using 24 blank cards write down the name of 12 cities and their time zone. Play snap. When a time and city match, players call out and collect the pair.

www.eyewitnesstohistory.com/wright.htm

The Airbus A380 is the largest passenger aeroplane in the world. It first came into service in 2007 and can carry 853 passengers.

Impact of air travel

New airports are being built around the world as more and more people want to travel by air. Airports take a lot of space. The noise and fumes from planes are also harming the environment. Do you think we can go on living like this?

World time zones

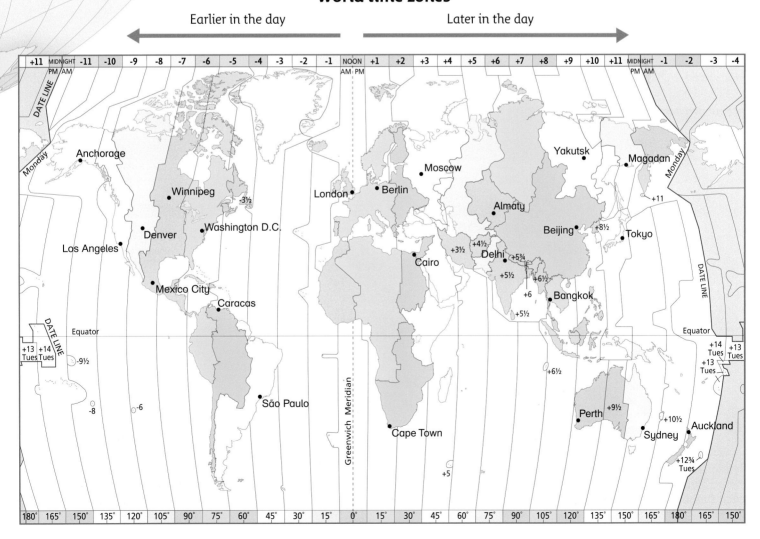

Mountains, Rivers and Oceans

What is the Earth's surface like?

Over two thirds of the Earth's surface is covered by seas and oceans. The rest is dry land.

Key

Land height above sea level (metres)

- over 5000
- 2000 – 5000
- 1000 – 2000
- 500 – 1000
- 200 – 500
- 0 – 200
- land below sea level

8848 ▲ Mountain height (metres)

∿ River

Lake

Ice cap

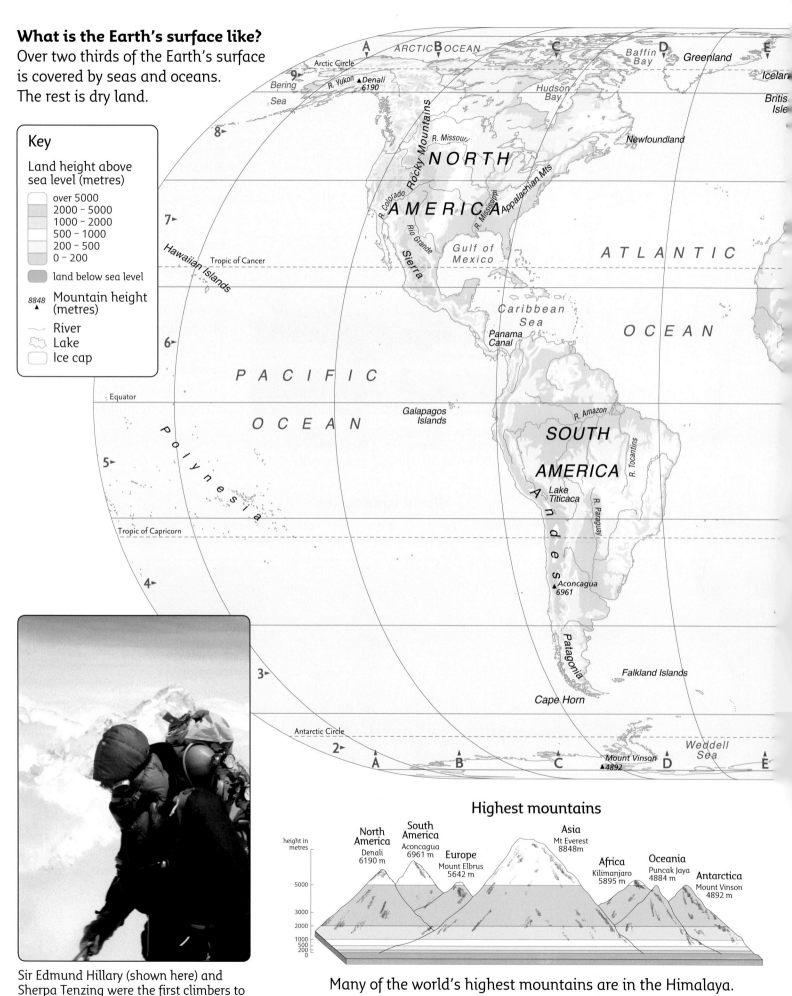

ARCTIC OCEAN

Arctic Circle

Bering Sea

R. Yukon ▲Denali 6190

Baffin Bay

Greenland

Hudson Bay

Icelan

Britis Isle

R. Missouri

NORTH AMERICA

Rocky Mountains

Appalachian Mts

R. Colorado

R. Mississippi

Newfoundland

Rio Grande

Sierra

Gulf of Mexico

ATLANTIC

Hawaiian Islands

Tropic of Cancer

Caribbean Sea

Panama Canal

OCEAN

PACIFIC

OCEAN

Equator

Galapagos Islands

R. Amazon

SOUTH AMERICA

R. Tocantins

Polynesia

Lake Titicaca

R. Paraguay

Andes

Tropic of Capricorn

Aconcagua 6961

Patagonia

Falkland Islands

Cape Horn

Antarctic Circle

Mount Vinson ▲4892

Weddell Sea

Highest mountains

height in metres

North America
Denali 6190 m

South America
Aconcagua 6961 m

Europe
Mount Elbrus 5642 m

Asia
Mt Everest 8848m

Africa
Kilimanjaro 5895 m

Oceania
Puncak Jaya 4884 m

Antarctica
Mount Vinson 4892 m

5000
3000
2000
1000
500
200
0

Many of the world's highest mountains are in the Himalaya. This diagram shows the highest peak in each continent.

Sir Edmund Hillary (shown here) and Sherpa Tenzing were the first climbers to reach the top of Mount Everest in 1953.

These images show two views of the surface of the Earth.

ASIA

PACIFIC OCEAN

What is a continent? (?)

A continent is a great block of land together with any nearby islands. There are seven continents in the world. Asia is the largest. Oceania is the smallest.

Longest rivers

Africa — Nile – 6695 km
South America — Amazon – 6516 km
Asia — Chang Jiang – 6380 km
North America — Mississippi-Missouri – 5969 km
Oceania — Murray-Darling – 3750 km
Europe — Volga – 3688 km

The Nile is the world's longest river. The Amazon is slightly shorter but carries much more water as it flows through the rainforest.

The Earth's surface

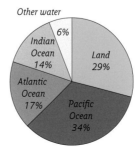

Other water 6%
Indian Ocean 14%
Land 29%
Atlantic Ocean 17%
Pacific Ocean 34%

The Pacific Ocean is nearly as large as all the other oceans put together.

Activities

➤ Make a fact file naming a mountain, river, lake and island in each continent apart from Antarctica.

➤ Discuss why people climb mountains. Make up a Mount Everest board game to play in class.

www.peakware.com
www.youtube.com (search for Mount Everest)

Volcanoes, Earthquakes and Storms

How are we affected by volcanoes, earthquakes and storms?

Earthquakes, volcanoes and storms affect people all over the world. The worst events cause lots of damage and kill or injure thousands of people.

What causes earthquakes and volcanoes? (?)

Beneath the Earth's surface there are red hot rocks. As these rocks move, they cause earthquakes on the surface. When they break through, they create volcanoes. This tends to happen near plate boundaries.

Activities

- Set up a notice board about disasters in the news.
- Choose a volcano. Now fold a sheet of A4 paper into four strips. Do a drawing, map, writing and data file about the volcano in each strip. Fix the sides together to make an open cube for a display.

http://volcano.oregonstate.edu

Arctic Circle

Aleutian Islands (2008)

Mt St Helens (1980)

San Francisco (1906)

NORTH AMERICA

Tropic of Cancer

Mexico City (1985)

Haiti (2010)

Nevado del Ruiz (1985)

Equator

PACIFIC OCEAN

Chimbote (1996)

SOUTH AMERICA

Tropic of Capricorn

Chile (2010)

Antarctic Circle

Eyjafjallajökull (2010)

Hekla (2000)

EUR

Vesuvi (167

Morocco (2004)

AFR

Lake Nyos (1986)

ATLANTIC OCEAN

A

Key

- **Earthquake**
- **Flood**
- **Volcano**
- **Drought**
- **Tornado**
- **Drought area**
- **Storm track**

Iceland 2010 Ash cloud
When a volcano (Eyjafjallajökull) erupted in Iceland in 2010 it sent a cloud of ash high in the air. Aircraft flights were cancelled across northern Europe in case there was a danger.

Japan 2011 Tsunami
In 2011 a powerful earthquake under the sea near Japan set off a tidal wave or tsunami. This caused terrible damage to Tohoku and other places along the coast, including a nuclear power station.

Nepal 2015 Earthquake
In 2015 a powerful earthquake destroy towns and villages across Nepal, killing thousands of people. It also triggered a massive avalanche on Mount Everest.

Major natural disasters

Date & place	Event	Deaths
1671 Italy	Vesuvius	60 000
1883 Indonesia	Krakatoa	36 000
1970 Bangladesh	Hurricane	750 000
1976 China (Tangshan)	Earthquake	242 000
1985 Colombia	Nevado del Ruiz	23 000
1990 Iran (Manjil)	Earthquake	50 000
1998 Caribbean Sea	Hurricane Mitch	15 000
2004 Indonesia (Aceh)	Tsunami	227 000
2005 Pakistan	Earthquake	75 000
2008 Myanmar	Cyclone Nargis	146 000
2008 China (Sichuan)	Earthquake	87 000
2010 Haiti	Earthquake	222 570
2011 Japan (Tohoku)	Tsunami	14 500
2013 Philippines	Typhoon Haiyan	6300
2015 Nepal	Earthquake	9000

Are natural hazards getting worse?

Volcanoes, earthquakes and storms are claiming more and more lives. This is partly because of the increasing number of people in the world. However, storms also seem to be getting more powerful. Scientists think this is due to climate change.

Measuring earthquakes

There are two scales for measuring earthquakes. The Richter scale measures the energy from the shock. The Mercalli scale measures the effect on people and buildings.

Plate boundaries

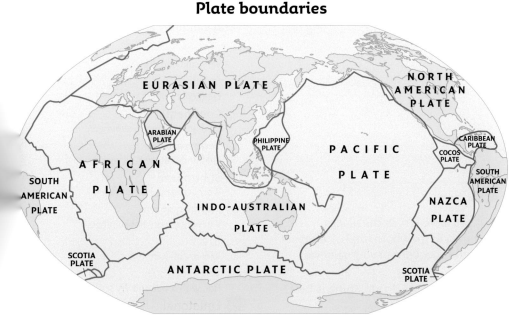

The Earth's crust is broken into great blocks called plates. These move very slowly in different directions.

Weather and Climate

What are the world's climates?

The mixture of rainfall and temperature from season to season makes the climate. There are many different climates. Places near the Equator are hot. Deserts are in the Tropics. Places near the Poles are cold. Damp air brings rain to places near the sea.

Polar climate
This is the coldest climate on Earth. Very few plants and animals can survive here.

Dry climate
In the desert, plants and animals have very little water.

Equatorial climate
It is always hot and wet here. There are huge numbers of plants and animals.

What is the difference between climate and weather? (?)

Weather happens from day to day. The climate is the pattern of the weather measured over 30 years.

Arctic Circle

Tropic of Cancer

Equator

Tropic of Capricorn

NORTH AMERICA

SOUTH AMERIC

Antarctic Circle

Activities

▸ If you were lost in the places shown in the photographs, what would you want in your survival kit?

▸ Which climate do you think is best?
www.bbc.co.uk/weather

Key
World climate

☐ Polar
Very cold and dry

☐ Subarctic
Long cold winters

☐ Continental
Cold winters, warm summers

☐ Temperate
Mild and quite wet all year

☐ Subtropical
Warm winters, hot summers

☐ Mediterranean
Wet winters, dry hot summers

☐ Dry
Very dry all year

☐ Tropical
Hot, with a wet and dry season

☐ Equatorial
Always hot and wet

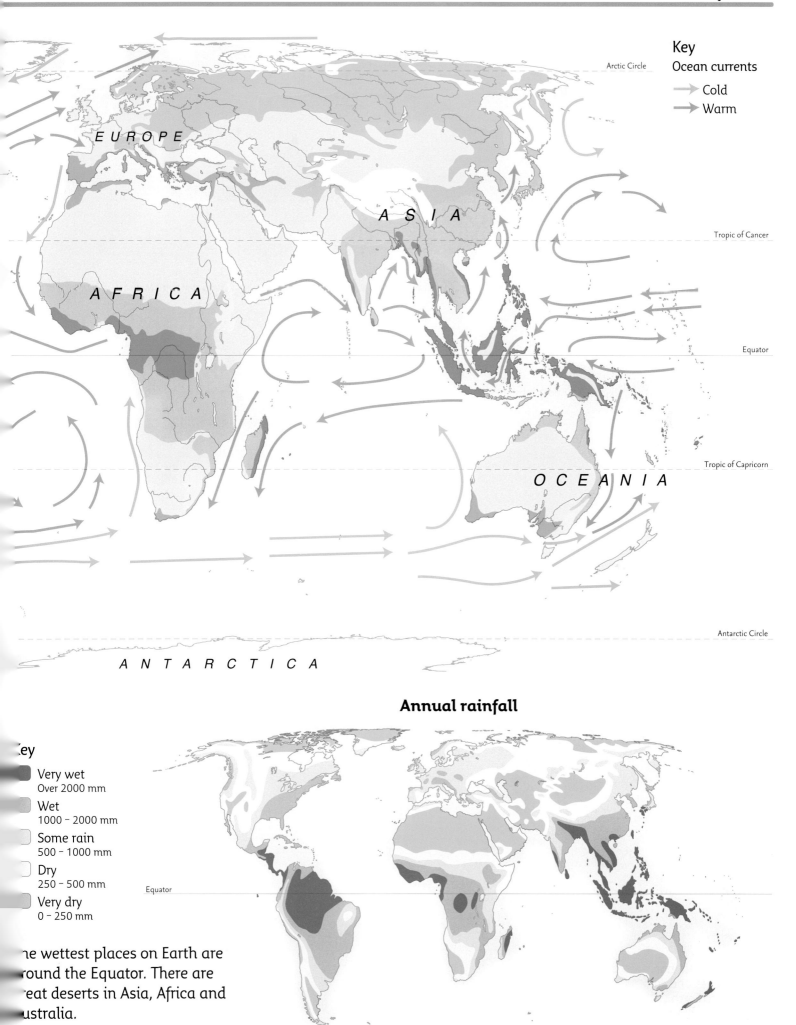

Arctic Circle

Key
Ocean currents
→ Cold
→ Warm

E U R O P E

A S I A

Tropic of Cancer

A F R I C A

Equator

Tropic of Capricorn

O C E A N I A

Antarctic Circle

A N T A R C T I C A

Annual rainfall

Key
■ **Very wet**
Over 2000 mm
■ **Wet**
1000 – 2000 mm
□ **Some rain**
500 – 1000 mm
□ **Dry**
250 – 500 mm
■ **Very dry**
0 – 250 mm

Equator

he wettest places on Earth are
round the Equator. There are
eat deserts in Asia, Africa and
ustralia.

Environmental Issues

How are we damaging our world?

There are now more people living in the world than ever before. People are also using more resources and creating more pollution than they did in the past. This is causing great changes to the balance of life.

Key

	Deserts
	Land that could become desert
	Rainforest
	Rainforest destroyed since 1940
	Oil slicks
★	Coral reefs at risk
●	Wildfires
◯	Plastic waste in the oceans

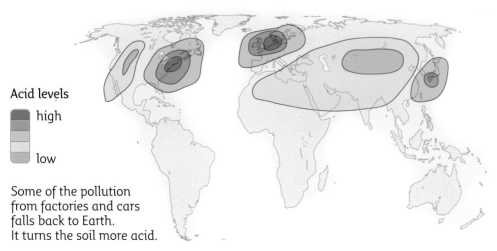

ARCTIC OCEAN

Arctic Circle

Rocky Mountains

NORTH AMERICA

Sierra Madre

ATLANTIC OCEAN

Tropic of Cancer

PACIFIC OCEAN

Equator

SOUTH AMERICA

Andes

Tropic of Capricorn

Activities

➤ How is the area where you live affected by pollution?

➤ Which of the issues shown on the map do you think is most serious and why?

www.bbc.co.uk/newsround/42810179

How does plastic pollution affect wildlife?

A lot of the plastic that we use ends up in the ocean. Some of it drifts round in huge pools carried by ocean currents. It also breaks down into little pieces that are carried all over the Earth. Many of the creatures that live in the sea, such as fish and sea birds, are being poisoned as a result.

Acid rain

Acid levels

high

low

Some of the pollution from factories and cars falls back to Earth. It turns the soil more acid.

Burning coal and other fossil fuels caus acid rain and global warming.

42

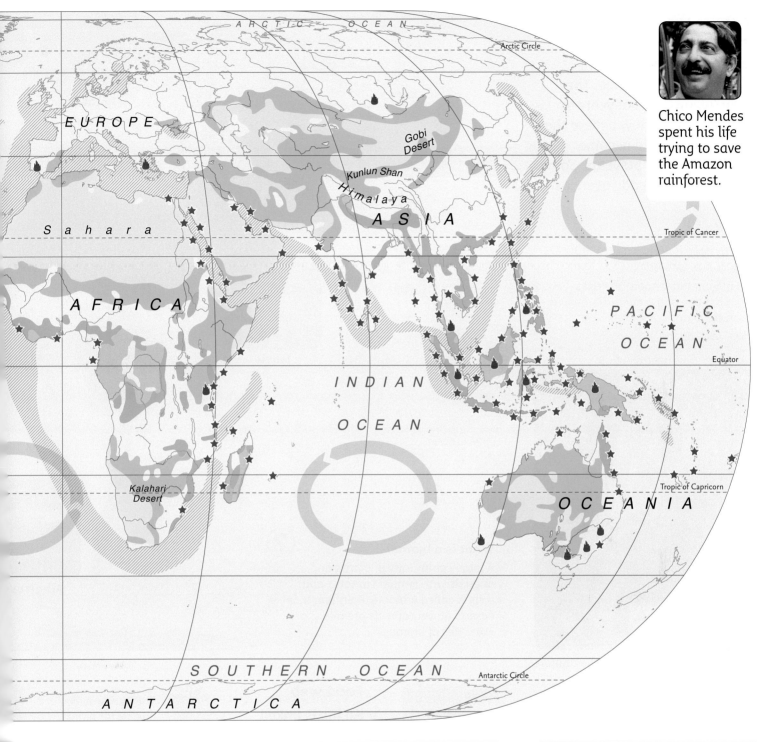

Chico Mendes spent his life trying to save the Amazon rainforest.

ısh fires are becoming more common Australia as the desert spreads.

The pool of rubbish in the Pacific Ocean is several times larger than the UK.

Habitats are destroyed when trees are cut down for industry and agriculture.

Wildlife at Risk

What are the dangers facing wildlife around the world?

Plants and creatures are the world's greatest resource. They have taken millions of years to evolve. Scientists now believe that many species could become extinct in the next 50 years. Some creatures have already been lost.

Activities

➤ Why does it matter if a creature becomes extinct?

➤ Find out more about the risks facing one of the creatures shown on the map.

www.wwf.org.uk

Plants and creatures thrive in the rainforest.

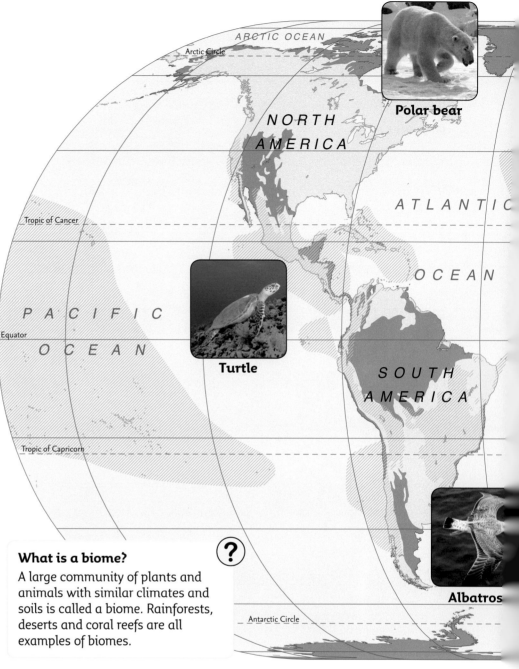

Polar bear

ARCTIC OCEAN

Arctic Circle

NORTH AMERICA

ATLANTIC

OCEAN

Tropic of Cancer

PACIFIC

Equator

OCEAN

Turtle

SOUTH AMERICA

Tropic of Capricorn

Albatros

Antarctic Circle

What is a biome?

A large community of plants and animals with similar climates and soils is called a biome. Rainforests, deserts and coral reefs are all examples of biomes.

Coral reefs support many different types of life.

Food web

All life is linked.

The sun provides energy for plants.

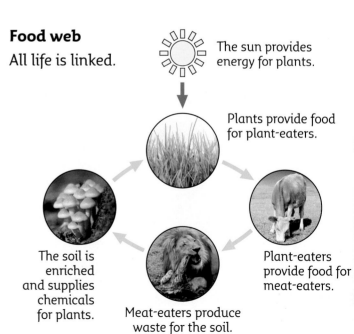

Plants provide food for plant-eaters.

The soil is enriched and supplies chemicals for plants.

Plant-eaters provide food for meat-eaters.

Meat-eaters produce waste for the soil.

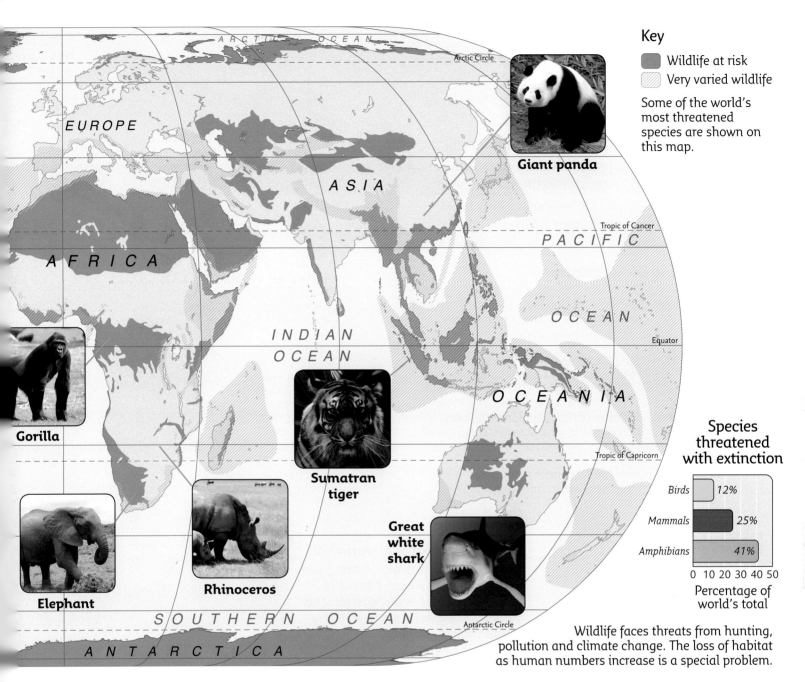

Key

- Wildlife at risk
- Very varied wildlife

Some of the world's most threatened species are shown on this map.

Giant panda

Gorilla

Sumatran tiger

Elephant

Rhinoceros

Great white shark

Species threatened with extinction

Birds	12%
Mammals	25%
Amphibians	41%

0 10 20 30 40 50
Percentage of world's total

Wildlife faces threats from hunting, pollution and climate change. The loss of habitat as human numbers increase is a special problem.

Tigers

In the past, tigers were hunted for their skins. Now the places where they used to live are being turned into farmland. It is not too late to save the tiger. Nature reserves have been set up to protect them. These have helped to halt the losses.

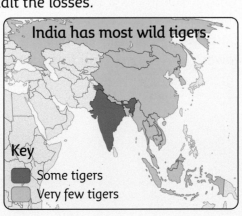

India has most wild tigers.

Key
- Some tigers
- Very few tigers

Tiger population

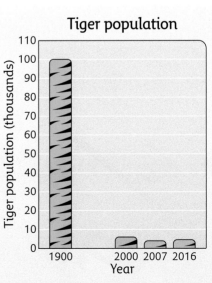

Tiger population (thousands)

110
100
90
80
70
60
50
40
30
20
10
0

1900   2000 2007 2016
Year

There are about 4000 tigers left in the wild and 1000 in zoos.

Climate Change

What is global warming?

Scientists now know that the world is getting warmer. They believe this is caused by air pollution. This change to the climate around the world is known as 'global warming'.

It is impossible to say how fast temperatures will rise or how people will be affected. Some plants and creatures will definitely become extinct. Poor people in the Tropics are likely to suffer most. Many have already become 'climate change refugees'.

Impact of rising temperatures

4 degrees	Many coasts flooded Sea levels rise as Antarctic ice melts
3 degrees	Amazon begins to turn to desert Millions of people made homeless
2 degrees	Collapse of the Greenland ice sheet Lots of plants and animals endangered
1 degree	Arctic sea ice melts in summer More heat waves and forest fires

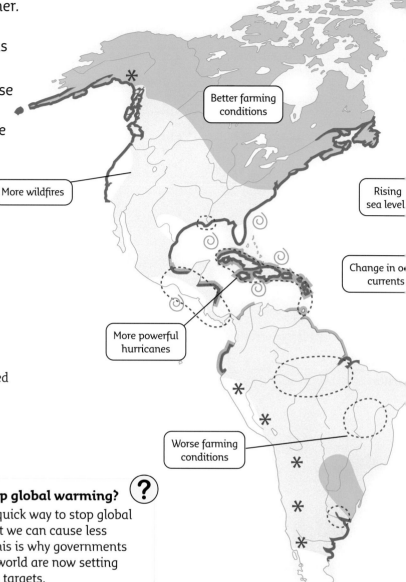

Better farming conditions

More wildfires

Rising sea level

Change in ocean currents

More powerful hurricanes

Worse farming conditions

Activities

➤ Who is likely to be most affected by global warming?

➤ Make up a poster about the causes and dangers of global warming.

www.greenpeace.org.uk/climate
https://se-ed.co.uk/edu

Can we stop global warming? (?)

There is no quick way to stop global warming but we can cause less pollution. This is why governments around the world are now setting air pollution targets.

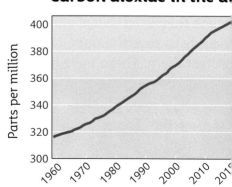

Greenhouse gases   Heat from the sun

Heat from the Earth

The Greenhouse Effect

Greenhouse gases stop heat bouncing back into space from the Earth's surface. Without these gases temperatures on Earth would be 20 or 30 degrees lower. Some people call this the 'greenhouse effect'.

Carbon dioxide in the ai[r]

Parts per million

400
380
360
340
320
300

1960 1970 1980 1990 2000 2010 201[0]

When we burn coal, oil, gas or wood we create carbon dioxide. This is one of the gases which causes the 'greenhouse eff[ect]'.

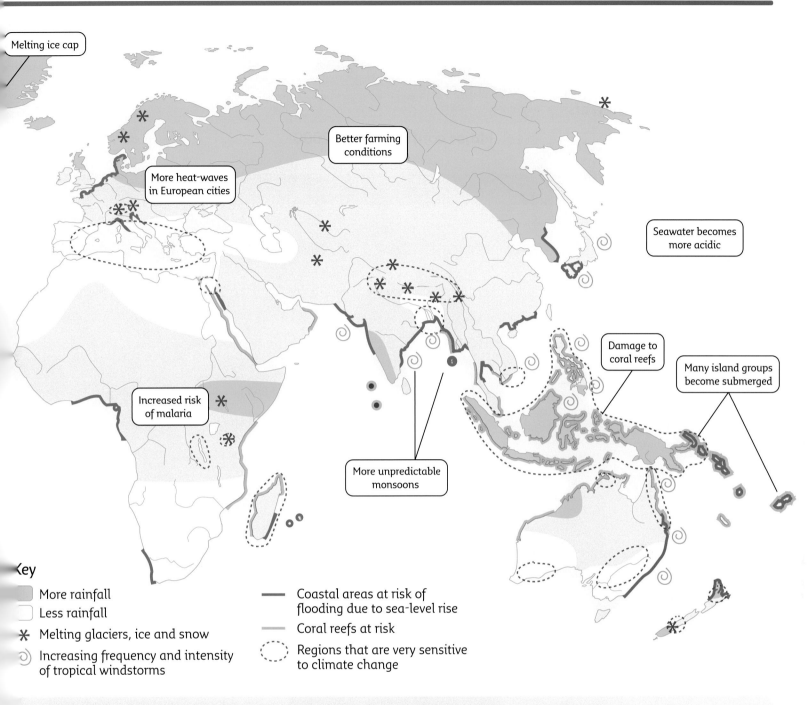

Melting ice cap

More heat-waves in European cities

Better farming conditions

Seawater becomes more acidic

Damage to coral reefs

Many island groups become submerged

Increased risk of malaria

More unpredictable monsoons

Key

- More rainfall
- Less rainfall
- * Melting glaciers, ice and snow
- ☺ Increasing frequency and intensity of tropical windstorms
- ━━ Coastal areas at risk of flooding due to sea-level rise
- ━━ Coral reefs at risk
- ⌒ Regions that are very sensitive to climate change

Shrinking glaciers

Glaciers advance and retreat over time. However, all around the world, glaciers, like this one at Aletsch in Switzerland, are retreating rapidly as a result of climate change.

War and Peace

Where in the world are there wars and conflicts?

We live in a violent world. There are conflicts in many parts of the world today. The map shows some of the worst hot spots in recent years.

Major conflicts since 2000

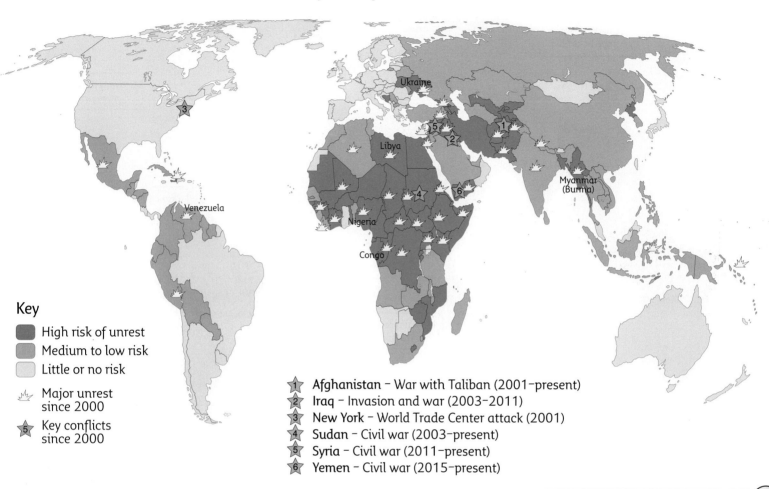

Key

- High risk of unrest
- Medium to low risk
- Little or no risk
- Major unrest since 2000
- Key conflicts since 2000

1. Afghanistan – War with Taliban (2001–present)
2. Iraq – Invasion and war (2003–2011)
3. New York – World Trade Center attack (2001)
4. Sudan – Civil war (2003–present)
5. Syria – Civil war (2011–present)
6. Yemen – Civil war (2015–present)

Antarctica World Park

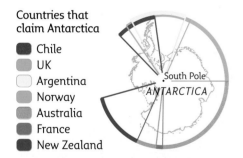

Countries that claim Antarctica

- Chile
- UK
- Argentina
- Norway
- Australia
- France
- New Zealand

Antarctica is the last great wilderness on Earth. It also has huge natural resources which are claimed by different countries. Antarctica was made into a world park in 1959. This has brought peace rather than conflict.

Nobel Peace Prize

The Nobel Peace Prize is awarded every year for great achievements. In 2014 the prize was won by Malala Yousafzai who campaigns for children's rights in her native country of Pakistan.

What is the United Nations?

The United Nations was set up in 1945 to help keep peace between nations. Sometimes it sends soldiers to keep two sides from fighting. It also works to improve living conditions and to see that people have good lives.

Activities

- Find out about the United Nations Convention on the Rights of the Child.
- Make a class display of maps, images and descriptions about the First or Second World War.

www.unicef.org

First World War 1914-1918

Millions of people lost their lives in the First World War. Some of the most dreadful battles were fought on the 'Western Front' in France. Here German soldiers fought against the French and British.

Stalemate between the armies led to bitter trench warfare.

Second World War 1939-1945

The Second World War broke out in Europe but ended up involving the USA, Japan and other countries around the world. Tanks, aircraft, submarines and machines were very important in fighting battles. In the areas ruled by Germany many Jews lost their lives.

r battles and bombing raids were an important part of the cond World War.

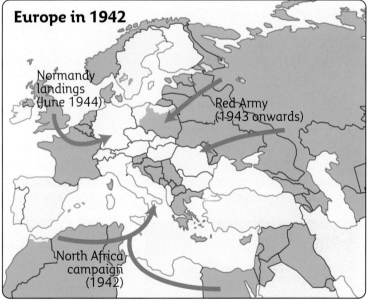

The Western Front

Route taken by German forces

Major battles

French fortresses

German attack plan

Franco-German border

* This map uses modern country boundaries

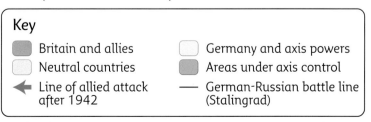

Europe in 1942

Normandy landings (June 1944)

Red Army (1943 onwards)

North Africa campaign (1942)

* The map above uses modern country boundaries

Key

Britain and allies	Germany and axis powers
Neutral countries	Areas under axis control
Line of allied attack after 1942	German-Russian battle line (Stalingrad)

In 1942 Germany and the axis powers had gained control of nearly all of mainland Europe.

🌐 Globalisation

What is globalisation?

The way that people around the world are linked together through communications, trade and travel is known as globalisation.

Globalisation started hundreds of years ago. Recently it has speeded up due to technology. People disagree about the benefits.

Activities

➤ Make a survey of where the food, clothes and other goods in and around your class were made.

➤ Find out more about the growth and decline of the British Empire and the impact that it has had on the world.

http://think-global.org.uk/

International trade

The goods we buy are often made in different places using materials from all over the world. Here is a list of countries involved in making a single pair of jeans.

1. China Cotton
2. Pakistan Soft cotton (pockets)
3. Italy Cloth (denim)
4. Germany Cotton dye
5. Namibia Copper for rivets
6. Australia Zinc for rivets
7. Japan Zip teeth
8. Turkey Pumice (stone washing)
9. Northern Ireland Thread (sewing)
10. Tunisia Clothes factory

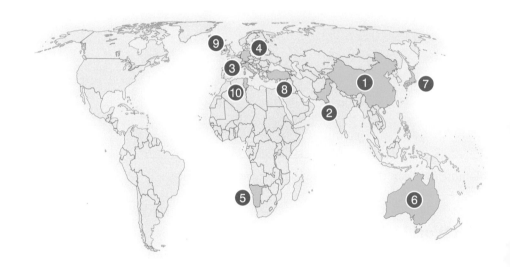

Globalisation involves links and connections

Messages

People use phones, emails and the internet to communicate with each other all over the world.

Billions of phone calls and internet messages are sent every day. Nobody knows exactly how many.

Factories

The raw materials used by factories often come from places thousands of kilometres away.

Oil from the Middle East is made into plastic, paint and other products in Europe and China.

Banks

Banks are linked to each other around the world through a complex system of loans and debts.

Millions of company shares are traded every day using money from different countries.

European Empires in 1900

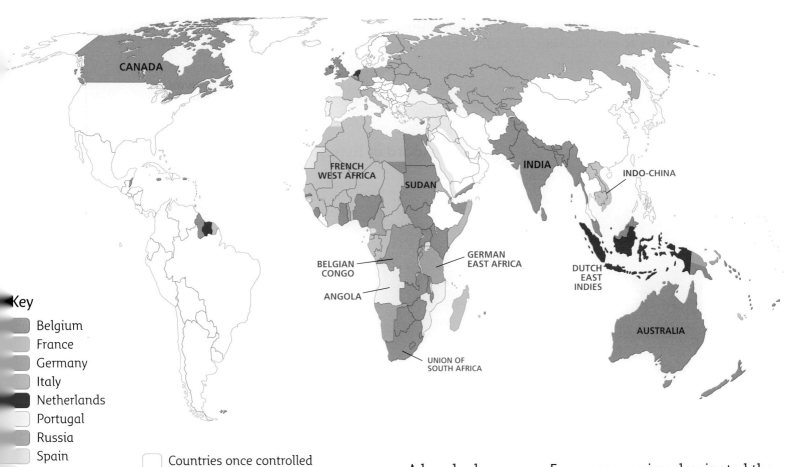

Key

- Belgium
- France
- Germany
- Italy
- Netherlands
- Portugal
- Russia
- Spain
- Ottoman Empire
- United Kingdom
- Countries once controlled by Europeans
- Other countries

* The map above uses modern country boundaries

A hundred years ago European empires dominated the world. The links that were set up between countries at that time are still important today.

Travel

Major cities are all linked together by aircraft making it possible to fly to places all over the world.

Over two billion people travel by air each year for business and tourism. Planes are also used for moving goods.

Language

More and more people are talking to each other in English even when it is not their first language.

There are over 7000 languages in the world today but many of these are dying out.

Environment

Environmental problems such as global warming and the loss of wildlife affect people wherever they may live.

Organisations like Greenpeace want people to think about the planet rather than just their own needs.

Ways of Living

What are the differences in living standards between countries?

All people have similar needs. We have to have food, clean water, shelter and security to survive. We want to be happy, live a long life and be part of a community. We also enjoy learning and using our skills. These things make up our quality of life.

Can we measure people's standard of living? ?

There are many ways of measuring people's quality of life. The map on this page puts three factors together:
  (1) money
  (2) length of life
  (3) education.

Standard of living

Key
- High
- Medium
- Low
- No data

Only 50% of Maasai children in Tanzania go to primary school.

The world family

Imagine there were only 100 people in the world. This diagram tells you about the people in that family.

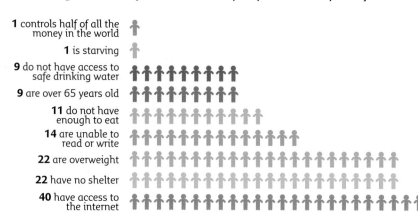

- **1** controls half of all the money in the world
- **1** is starving
- **9** do not have access to safe drinking water
- **9** are over 65 years old
- **11** do not have enough to eat
- **14** are unable to read or write
- **22** are overweight
- **22** have no shelter
- **40** have access to the internet

Activities

➤ Using information from this double page, discuss what you think makes people happy.

➤ Make a list of (a) your hopes and (b) your fears for the world in the years to come.

www.wwf.org.uk

Easter Island

Easter Island is in the Pacific Ocean thousands of kilometres from land. In the past the people who lived here grew rich and built great statues. However, as human numbers increased food became scarce and the trees were cut down. People began to fight for resources. When Captain Cook landed in 1774 he found just a few people left living miserable lives.

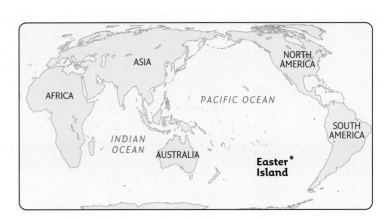

There are hundreds of stone statues on Easter Island.

Easter Island

Key

Land height above sea level (metres)
- over 500
- 200 – 500
- 0 – 200

507 ▲ Mountain height (metres)

Ecological footprint

The amount of land needed to provide all the food, clothing and resources we use is known as our 'ecological footprint'. The diagram shows that we now demand much more from the Earth than it can provide. This is partly because there are more and more people and partly because we are all consuming more.

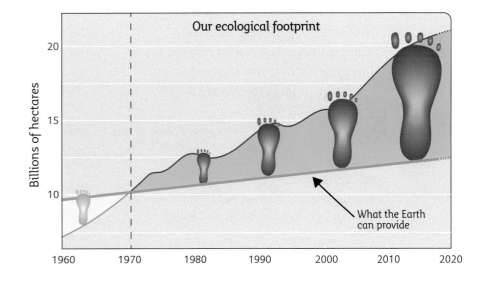

Sustainable Development Goals

In 2015 the United Nations agreed on a plan which aims to end poverty, protect the planet and create peace and prosperity. There are 17 goals to be achieved by 2030. These goals are known as the Sustainable Development Goals. They will guide people as they seek to create a better future.

Glossary

Antarctic	Area around the South Pole with very low temperatures
Arctic	Area around the North Pole with very low temperatures
Atlas	A book of maps
Biome	A biome is a global community of plants and animals. There are four main land biomes – forest, grassland, desert and tundra
Capital city	The city where a country's laws and decisions are made
Civilisation	The beliefs and achievements of a country or empire over a long period of time
Climate	The pattern of weather over many years
Community	A group of people who share the same ideas and beliefs
Compass	A device which uses a magnetic needle for finding compass directions
Conservation	Caring for the environment
Continent	A great block of land like Africa and nearby islands
Coral	Sea creatures with hard skeletons that build reefs in warm seas
Country	A territory with its own laws and flag
Crater	A sunken area at the top of a volcano
Crops	The plants that people grow to eat
Desert	A part of the Earth with a very dry climate
Earth	The name for the planet that we live on
Earthquake	Violent cracking and shaking of the Earth's surface
Environment	Our surroundings, especially plants and creatures
Environmental	The food, water and other resources needed to sustain our daily life
Equator	An imaginary line round the Earth, halfway between the North and South poles
Fair trade	Fair trade goods are produced in reasonable conditions by workers who get a fair wage
Food chain	The way all plants and creatures depend on each other in a web of life
Glacier	A great river of ice that moves slowly down a slope
Globalisation	The way people around the world are linked together by trade and communications
Global warming	Warming of the climate around the world
Greenhouse effect	The heating of the Earth caused by air pollution
Greenwich Meridian	Imaginary line from the North Pole to the South Pole passing through London (Greenwich) from which time is measured

Habitat	The environment that suits a particular set of plants and creatures
Hurricane	Violent storm found only in the tropics
Latitude	Imaginary lines that go round the Earth in hoops parallel to the Equator
Lava	Molten/Red hot rock that flows from a volcano when it erupts
Longitude	Imaginary lines that go from the North Pole to the South Pole
Map projection	The system used by a map maker to draw maps of the world or continents
Monsoon rains	Rains which come after the dry season in southeast Asia
Natural hazard	Events like earthquakes which happen naturally and which can harm people
Nature reserve	An area or region set aside for wildlife
Ocean	Large mass of deep seawater
Ore	Rock which contains metal and other materials
Planet	The Earth is one of eight planets that orbit the sun
Pollution	Fumes, noise and waste which damage our surroundings and harm our health
Population	The number of people or creatures in a place
Rainforest	Forest which grows in hot, wet climates
Region	An area such as a river basin or mountain range which has something in common
Resources	The things we get from the ground or sea
Route	The way we go from one place to another
Satellite image	Photograph of the Earth's surface taken by satellite
Sea	An area of shallow seawater found at the edge of a continent
Sustainable living	Living in a way that gives back to the Earth as much as we take out
Trade	The exchange of goods, money and services between people and countries
Tropics	Areas of the Earth where the sun is directly overhead at some point in the year
Tsunami	Great waves caused by an earthquake
Volcano	Place (often a mountain) where red hot rocks come to the surface from deep underground
Weather	The day to day mixture of sun, wind, rain and snow
United Nations	Organisation open to all countries of the world, set up to keep peace and improve life

The list of names, or Index, on this page and page 56, includes many of the names on the maps.

The names in the Index are arranged in alphabetical order. In each line the name of the feature is given first. If required, e.g. Yukon river, there is a description before the page number, such as river, state or country. The page number is followed by a grid letter and number. For example: Yukon *river* 36 A9

To use the Index to locate a name in the atlas, first find the name in the Index and note the page number and grid reference. Then turn to the correct page in the atlas. Find the grid letters at the bottom of the map and put your finger on the letter given in the grid reference. Now find the correct grid number at the side of the map. Move your fingers along the number row and up the letter column until they meet in the same square. The name you are looking for will be in this square.

In this index cities and towns are shown in green, water features in blue, countries and states in red and physical features in black.

A

Abidjan *town* 12 B3
Abuja *capital* 12 C3
Accra *capital* 12 B3
Aconcagua *mountain* 19
Addis Ababa *capital* 12 D3
Adelaide *town* 20 C2
Aden *town* 14 B2
Adriatic Sea 8 E2
Aegean Sea 8 F1
Afghanistan *country* 14 C3
Africa *continent* 12-13
Alaska *state* 16 B4
Albania *country* 8 E2
Alexandria *town* 12 D4
Algeria *country* 12 B4
Algiers *capital* 12 C4
Alice Springs *town* 20 C3
Almaty *town* 14 D4
Alps *mountains* 9
Altai Mountains 15
Amazon *river* 19
Amazon Basin 19
American Samoa *territory* 6 A5
Amur *river* 37 I8
Anchorage *town* 16 B4
Andes *mountains* 19
Andorra *country* 8 D2
Angola *country* 12 C2
Ankara *capital* 14 B3
Antananarivo *capital* 12 E2
Antarctica *continent* 23
Antigua and Barbuda *country* 16 F1
Antofagasta *town* 18 B3
Aoraki/Mount Cook 20
Appalachian Mountains 36 C7
Arabian Peninsula 15
Arabian Sea 14 C2
Aracaju *town* 18 D4
Arafura Sea 20 C4
Aral Sea 14 C4
Arctic Ocean 36 B9
Arequipa *town* 18 B4
Argentina *country* 18 B2
Armenia *country* 14 B4
Ashgabat *capital* 14 C3
Asia *continent* 14-15
Asmara *capital* 12 D3
Astana *capital* 14 D4
Asunción *capital* 18 C3
Athens *capital* 8 F1
Atlanta *town* 16 E2
Atlantic Ocean 36 D7
Atlas Mountains 13
Auckland *town* 20 G2
Australia *country* 20 B3
Austria *country* 8 E2
Ayers Rock *see* Uluru/Ayers Rock
Azerbaijan *country* 14 B4
Baffin Bay 16 F4
Baffin Island 22
Baghdad *capital* 14 B3
Bahrain *country* 14 C3
Balearic Islands 8 D1

Baltic Sea 8 E3
Bamako *capital* 12 B3
Bangkok *capital* 14 E2
Bangladesh *country* 14 D3
Bangui *capital* 12 C3
Barbados *country* 16 G1
Barcelona *town* 8 D2
Barents Sea 22
Barranquilla *town* 18 B5
Bay of Bengal 14 D2
Bay of Biscay 8 C2
Beaufort Sea 22
Beijing *capital* 14 F4
Beira *town* 12 D2
Belarus *country* 8 F3
Belém *town* 18 C4
Belfast *town* 8 C3
Belgium *country* 8 D3
Belgrade *capital* 8 F2
Belize *country* 16 E1
Belo Horizonte *town* 18 C4
Benghazi *town* 12 D4
Benin *country* 12 C3
Bering Sea 22
Berlin *capital* 8 E3
Bermuda *territory* 16 F2
Bhutan *country* 14 D3
Black Sea 8 G2
Bloemfontein *capital* 12 D1
Bogotá *capital* 18 B5
Bolivia *country* 18 B4
Borneo *island* 14 F1
Bosnia and Herzegovina *country* 8 E2
Boston *town* 16 F3
Botswana *country* 12 D1
Brasília *capital* 18 C4
Bratislava *capital* 8 E2
Brazil *country* 18 B4
Brazilian Highlands 19
Brazzaville *capital* 12 C2
Brisbane *town* 20 E3
British Isles *islands* 36 E8
Brooks Range *mountains* 22
Brunei *country* 14 F2
Bucharest *capital* 8 F2
Budapest *capital* 8 E2
Buenos Aires *capital* 18 C3
Bulgaria *country* 8 F2
Burkina Faso *country* 12 B3
Burma *see* Myanmar
Burundi *country* 12 D2

C

Cairns *town* 20 D4
Cairo *capital* 12 D4
Calgary *town* 16 D3
Cali *town* 18 B5
Cambodia *country* 14 E2
Cameroon *country* 12 C3
Canada *country* 16 D3
Canary Islands 12 B4
Canberra *capital* 20 D2
Cape Horn 36 D3
Cape of Good Hope 37 F4
Cape Town *capital* 12 C1
Cape Verde *country* 12 A3
Caracas *capital* 18 B5

Caribbean Sea 16 F1
Carpathian Mountains 9
Casablanca *town* 12 B4
Caspian Sea 14 C3
Caucasus *mountains* 9
Cayenne *capital* 18 C5
Celebes *island* 14 F1
Central African Republic *country* 12 C3
Central Siberian Plateau 22
Chad *country* 12 C3
Chang Jiang *river* 15
Chelyabinsk *town* 14 C4
Chennai *town* 14 D2
Chicago *town* 16 E3
Chile *country* 18 B3
China *country* 14 D3
Chişinău *capital* 8 F2
Chongqing *town* 14 E3
Christchurch *town* 20 G1
Colombia *country* 18 B5
Colombo *town* 14 D2
Colorado *river* 36 C7
Comoros *country* 12 E2
Conakry *capital* 12 B3
Concepción *town* 18 B3
Congo *country* 12 C2
Congo *river* 13
Cook Islands 6 A5
Copenhagen *capital* 8 E3
Coral Sea 20 E4
Corsica *island* 8 D2
Costa Rica *country* 16 E1
Côte d'Ivoire *country* 12 B3
Crete *island* 8 F1
Croatia *country* 8 E2
Cuba *country* 16 F2
Curitiba *town* 18 C3
Cyprus *country* 14 B3
Czechia *country* 8 E2

D

Dakar *capital* 12 B3
Dallas *town* 16 E2
Danube *river* 9
Dar es Salaam *town* 12 D2
Darling *river* 20
Darwin *town* 20 C4
Davao *town* 14 F2
Delhi *town* 14 D3
Democratic Republic of the Congo *country* 12 D3
Denali *mountain* 17
Denmark *country* 8 D3
Denver *town* 16 D2
Detroit *town* 16 E3
Dhaka *capital* 14 E3
Dili *capital* 14 F1
Djibouti *capital* 12 E3
Djibouti *country* 12 E3
Dodoma *capital* 12 D2
Dominica *country* 16 F1
Dominican Republic *country* 16 F1
Drakensberg *mountains* 37 F4
Dublin *capital* 8 C3
Dunedin *town* 20 F1

E

East China Sea 37 I7
East Siberian Sea 22
East Timor (Timor-Leste) *country* 14 F1
Ecuador *country* 18 B4
Edinburgh *town* 8 C3
Edmonton *town* 16 D3
Egypt *country* 12 D4
El Paso *town* 16 D2
El Salvador *country* 16 E1
English Channel 8 C2
Equatorial Guinea *country* 12 C3
Eritrea *country* 12 D3
Estonia *country* 8 F3
Eswatini *country* 12 D1
Ethiopia *country* 12 D3
Ethiopian Highlands 13
Euphrates *river* 15
Europe *continent* 8-11

F

Falkland Islands 18 C2
Faroe Islands 8 C4
Federated States of Micronesia *country* 7 I6
Fiji *country* 20 G4
Finland *country* 8 F4
Fortaleza *town* 18 D4
France *country* 8 C2
Freetown *capital* 12 B3
French Guiana *territory* 18 C5
Fukuoka *town* 14 G3

G

Gabon *country* 12 C2
Gaborone *capital* 12 D1
Galapagos Islands 18 A4
Ganges *river* 15
Geelong *town* 20 D2
Georgetown *capital* 18 C5
Georgia *country* 14 B4
Germany *country* 8 D3
Ghana *country* 12 B3
Gibraltar *town* 8 C1
Giza *town* 12 D4
Gobi Desert 15
Gold Coast *town* 20 E3
Grand Canyon 17
Great Australian Bight *bay* 20 C2
Great Barrier Reef 20
Great Bear Lake 16 D4
Great Dividing Range *mountains* 20
Great Lakes 17
Great Sandy Desert 20
Great Slave Lake 16 D4
Great Victoria Desert 20
Greece *country* 8 F1
Greenland *territory* 16 G4
Grenada *country* 16 F1
Guadalajara *town* 16 D2
Guangzhou *town* 14 F3
Guatemala *country* 16 E1
Guatemala City *capital* 16 E1
Guayaquil *town* 18 B4
Guinea *country* 12 B3
Guinea Bissau *country* 12 B3

H

Gulf of Bothnia 8 E4
Gulf of Mexico 16 E2
Guyana *country* 18 C5

Haiti *country* 16 F1
Halifax *town* 16 F3
Hanoi *capital* 14 E3
Harare *capital* 12 D2
Harbin *town* 14 F4
Havana *capital* 16 E2
Helsinki *capital* 8 F4
Himalaya *mountains* 15
Hobart *town* 20 D1
Ho Chi Minh City *town* 14 E2
Honduras *country* 16 E1
Hong Kong *town* 14 F3
Honiara *capital* 20 E4
Honshu *island* 37 I7
Houston *town* 16 E2
Huang He *river* 15
Hudson Bay 16 E4
Hungary *country* 8 E2
Hyderabad *town* 14 D2

I

Iceland *country* 8 A4
India *country* 14 D3
Indian Ocean 37 G5
Indonesia *country* 14 E1
Indus *river* 15
Iquitos *town* 18 B4
Iran *country* 14 B3
Iraq *country* 14 B3
Ireland *country* 8 C3
Irkutsk *town* 14 E4
Islamabad *capital* 14 D3
Israel *country* 14 B3
İstanbul *town* 8 F2
Italy *country* 8 E2

J

Jakarta *capital* 14 E1
Jamaica *country* 16 F1
Japan *country* 14 G3
Java *island* 14 E1
Johannesburg *town* 12 D1
Jordan *country* 14 B3
Juba *capital* 12 D3

K

K2 *mountain* 15
Kabul *capital* 14 C3
Kalahari Desert 13
Kalgoorlie *town* 20 B2
Kampala *capital* 12 D3
Kansas City *town* 16 E2
Karachi *town* 14 C3
Kara Sea 22
Kati Thanda-Lake Eyre 20 C3
Kazakhstan *country* 14 C4
Kenya *country* 12 D3
Khartoum *capital* 12 D3
Kiev *capital* 8 G3
Kilimanjaro *mountain* 13
Kingston *capital* 16 F1
Kinshasa *capital* 12 C2
Kiribati *country* 20 G5

Index